Bounded Rationality and Behavioural Economics

T0330907

In the last forty years there has been an astonishing surge in our understanding of how people make economic decisions. This book examines the evolution of the two fields credited with such advances: behavioural economics and bounded rationality.

Bounded rationality and behavioural economics both emerged from discontent with the descriptive and predictive power of the standard model of rational choice. However, they have evolved along increasingly divergent paths. This book examines the commonalities and differences of each stream of thought, as well as the consequences of their divergence. It culminates in the presentation of a new approach to the analysis of economic decision-making to address the fundamental criticism of these fields, requiring them to engage in greater collaboration.

This book calls for a re-fusion of bounded rationality and behavioural economics, and will be of interest to both students and researchers.

Graham Mallard is the Head of Economics at Cheltenham College and a Visiting Research Fellow at the University of Bath, UK.

Routledge Advances in Behavioural Economics and Finance
Edited by Richard Fairchild
University of Bath, UK

Bounded Rationality and Behavioural Economics

Graham Mallard

Routledge
Taylor & Francis Group

LONDON AND NEW YORK

First published 2016
by Routledge
2 Park Square, Milton Park, Abingdon, Oxon OX14 4RN

and by Routledge
711 Third Avenue, New York, NY 10017

First issued in paperback 2018

Routledge is an imprint of the Taylor & Francis Group, an informa business

British Library Cataloguing in Publication Data
A catalogue record for this book is available from the British Library

Library of Congress Cataloging in Publication Data
Mallard, Graham, 1982-
Bounded rationality and behavioural economics / Graham Mallard.
pages cm
Includes bibliographical references and index.
1. Economics--Psychological aspects. 2. Rational expectations (Economic
theory) I. Title.
HB74.P8M36 2015
330.01'9--dc23
2015009809

ISBN 13: 978-1-138-49974-4 (pbk)
ISBN 13: 978-1-138-79020-9 (hbk)

Typeset in Times New Roman
by Fish Books Ltd.

For Fay, Oculi, Omni and Monnie:
who keep me as rational as I am

Contents

Illustrations

Figures

Tables

1 Behavioural economics and bounded rationality

The discipline of political economy (or 'economics', as it has been known since the turn of the twentieth century) has always overlapped with that of psychology. Indeed, being the 'science which studies human behavior as a relationship between given ends and scarce means which have alternative uses' (Robbins, 1932: 16), this overlap is unavoidable. Avineri (2012), for example, argues that in his *Theory of Moral Sentiments* (1759), Adam Smith asserted the importance of psychological insights for understanding individual economic behaviour, including notions such as habits and customs, and also concerns about social wealth, fairness and justice. Then in March 1979, with the publication of the article 'Prospect theory: an analysis of decision under risk' by Daniel Kahneman and Amos Tversky, this overlap between these two disciplines experienced a dramatic turn: it became a field of study in its own right and the discipline of behavioural economics was born, which focuses explicitly on the study of economic decision-making and on issues such as those raised 150 years ago by the founder of modern economics. Only four years later, the first conference dedicated specifically to the new field was held at Princeton University (Frantz, 2004), securing its place in the economics discipline.

Over the past thirty-five years, and particularly in the last decade, behavioural economics has experienced astonishing growth as a separate field of economics. Earl (2005) identifies four indicators of this growth:

1   That two *Sveriges Riksbank Prizes in Economic Sciences in Memory of Alfred Nobel* (Nobel Prizes) have been awarded to academics working in this field (Herbert Simon in 1978 and Daniel Kahneman in 2002); although Frantz (2004) claims that those awarded to George Akerlof and Joseph Stiglitz in 2001 were also for works of behavioural economics.
2   The rapid expansion of the literature: Burnham (2013) observes that there now exist in excess of 50,000 papers that cite the works of Kahneman and Tversky (1979) and Tversky and Kahneman (1974), making a comprehensive examination of the field almost impossible.
3   The growth in the number of academic societies and journals that are devoted to the field, including the *International Association for Research in Economic Psychology*, the *Society for the Advancement of Socio-Economics* and the *Society for the Advancement of Behavioural Economics*; and the *Journal of*

Economic Psychology, the *Journal of Socio-Economics* and the *Journal of Economic Behavior and Organisation*, respectively.

4   That numerous economists working in the field have been hired by leading United States universities (and those across the world), along with the media attention that the field has enjoyed, perhaps most notably the *New York Times* article on 11 February 2001 by Uchitelle.

Further evidence of this growth lies in the fact that, because of its appeal to pre-university students (the 'Ariely effect'), it is the only new field being included in three of the four largest further-education economics specifications in the United Kingdom, which are being revised for 2015 onwards.

However, the course on which the development of behavioural economics is being steered is curious and possibly concerning. Predating the seminal work by Kahneman and Tversky by two decades, Herbert Simon developed the concept of 'bounded rationality'. This asserts that the cognitive abilities of human decision-makers are not always sufficient to find optimal solutions to complex real-life problems, leading decision-makers to find satisfactory, suboptimal outcomes. Simon's work was a foundational component of the development of behavioural economics as a field in its own right, but despite receiving the Nobel Prize for economics in 1978 for 'his pioneering research into the decision-making process within economic organizations' (Nobelprize.org), Simon's work has of late been, at least partially, overlooked in the behavioural economics literature. For instance, the aforementioned *New York Times* article by Uchitelle failed to refer to either Simon or his work.

The fields of behavioural economics and bounded rationality, even though they both emerged due to discontent with the descriptive and predictive power of the standard economics model of rational choice, have evolved in different directions, each with its own literature, its own approach and its own proponents. As will be further elucidated below, the former is concerned with the integration of methodology from psychology into economics analysis, whereas the latter largely analyses the implications of suboptimal decision-making through the mathematically sophisticated methodology of mainstream economics. The purpose of this research monograph is to examine the nature, the consequences and the advantages and the disadvantages of these different evolutionary paths, and to identify avenues of research in economics that would benefit from a re-fusion of these two fields. In particular, the intention is for this monograph to address four issues:

1   The nature of the different evolutionary paths of the literatures of behavioural economics and bounded rationality. For example, the intention is to answer questions such as: With what issues are they each concerned? What approaches to their studies do they each employ? Who are the primary audiences of each? And what are the areas of commonality and difference between them, in terms of their focus, methodologies and applications?

2   The consequences of this evolutionary divide. In terms of the areas of focus that are common across these two fields, to what extent do they lead to

compatible conclusions? Do the methodologies employed in each literature naturally lead to different outcomes and, if they do, what is the significance of this?

3   The advantages and disadvantages for economics as a whole of these two fields evolving in the different directions they have taken. To what extent is the specialisation that has occurred positive for, and to what degree is it impeding the development of, the wider subject?

4   The lessons that can be taken from an assessment of all of the above. Should this increasing divergence be promoted or counteracted, and are there areas of research for which a re-fusion of these literatures and approaches would be beneficial?

Behavioural economics

It is not at all clear at first glance what is meant by 'behavioural economics'. As noted above, it certainly occupies space within the area of overlap between the disciplines of economics and psychology. However, that area is vast and consists of a literature composed of a whole array of different methodological approaches, applied to an even larger array of questions and concerns. This is illustrated in Figure 1.1.

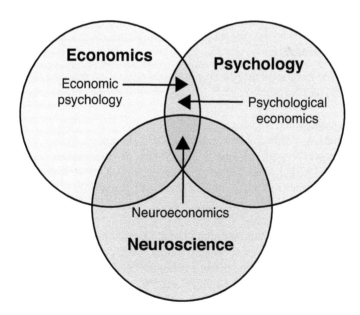

Figure 1.1 The nature of behavioural economics and bounded rationality

Earl (2005) suggests that there are two general approaches within this area of overlap between economics and psychology, an assertion that is supported by Fetchenhauer *et al.* (2012). The first is that of studies that seek to apply economic methodology and reasoning to issues that have traditionally been considered to be within the domain of psychology. They can be seen to be extending the realm of economics and can be labelled as studies of *economic psychology*. The quintessential example of such work is that of Becker, who employed the framework of neoclassical economics to analyse issues that were not traditionally economic in nature, including drug addiction, the family, and marriage and divorce. The second is that of studies that seek to apply methods and reasoning from psychology to issues that have traditionally been viewed as being the subject matter of economics. These can be seen to be extending the realm of psychology and so can be labelled as studies in *psychological economics*. In addition to these, there also exists the influence of neuroeconomics, which consists of studies that seek to apply the techniques of neuroscience to the analysis of economic issues: the 'brain studies', which 'monitor brain activity during decision making' (Rubinstein, 2007: 1244) (for a survey of this field see Camerer, 2007, which discusses the implications of neuroeconomics for economics, particularly in terms of the strengths that it has identified of the standard model of rational choice and the approaches of behavioural economics).

Following the judgement by Earl (2005), behavioural economics is taken to refer to the field of psychological economics: a field that 'seeks to use inputs from psychology to obtain an enhanced understanding of, and/or an improved ability to predict, behavior in respect of areas that have normally been viewed as the preserve of economics' (Earl, 2005: 911).

Bounded rationality

Simon (1955: 99) argues that the standard model of rational choice assumes that a decision-maker possesses:

> knowledge of the relevant aspects of his environment which, if not absolutely complete, is at least impressively clear and voluminous. He is assumed also to have a well-organized and stable system of preferences, and a skill in computation that enables him to calculate, for the alternative courses of action that are available to him, which of these will permit him to reach the highest attainable point on his preference scale.

Doubting the realism of this assumption of global, or objective, rationality, Simon repeatedly asserts that, 'as soon as we turn from very broad macroeconomic problems and wish to examine in some detail the behavior of the individual actors, difficulties begin to arise on all sides' (1957: 197). As an alternative, Simon proposes the principle of bounded rationality, which models decision-makers as being unable, most of the time, to identify, assimilate and process information in an optimising manner: 'the capacity of the human mind for formulating and solving complex problems is very small compared with the size of the problems whose solution is required for objectively rational behavior in the real world – or even for a reasonable approximation to such objective rationality' (1957: 198). With cognitive abilities not equal to the complexity of the decisions they have to make, decision-makers cannot optimise objective functions and so, by necessity, employ alternative cognitive strategies to make decisions. Indeed, decision-makers search for satisfactory outcomes by applying 'rules of thumb, or heuristics, to determine what paths should be traced and what ones can be ignored' and that the 'search halts when a satisfactory solution has been found, almost always long before all alternatives have been examined' (Simon *et al.*, 1992: 4). The first part of this, that decision-makers do not always possess cognitive capacities equal to the complexity of decisions they face (what Heiner, 1983, has termed the 'C-D gap') and so are unable to make decisions optimally, is the principle of *bounded rationality*. The second aspect (that they consequently search for a satisfactory outcome when making decisions) is the concept of *satisficing*.

Working in collaboration with Charles Holt and Franco Modigliani on the project 'Planning and Control of Industrial Operations' at the Graduate School of Industrial Administration of the Carnegie Institute of Technology, Herbert Simon and John Muth arrived at diametrically opposite views about decision-making within economic organisations: bounded rationality and rational expectations, respectively. While the former asserts that decision-makers do not always possess the capacity to make decisions optimally, the latter asserts that 'economists and the agents they are modeling should be placed on an equal footing: the agent in the model should be able to forecast and profit-maximize and utility-maximize as well as the economist – or should we say econometrician – who constructed the model' (Sargent, 1993: 21). The former leads to the conclusion that decision-makers inevitably settle for outcomes that are 'just good enough', whereas the latter leads to the conclusion that they are able to construct forecasts about economic data that contain no systematic error whatsoever.

The economics profession has favoured the rational expectations view and has, at various times and in various forms, sought to sideline Simon's alternative of bounded rationality. Perhaps inevitably given it was the birthplace of both bounded rationality and rational expectations, Simon arguably found his greatest critics within his own economics department at the Carnegie Institute of Technology: opposition that at least partially contributed to his decision to relocate to the Psychology Department (see Sent, 1997). Despite having received the Nobel Prize in 1978, Simon later lamented, 'my economist friends have long since given up on me, consigning me to psychology or some other distant wasteland' (1991: 385). It appears that this is continuing, with bounded rationality being sidelined or consigned to footnotes in the burgeoning behavioural economics literature.

Returning to the categorisation of Earl (2005), then, bounded rationality in the sense that Herbert Simon intended – based on suboptimal decision-making and satisficing – can be seen to also be within the field of psychological economics (indeed, psychologists often claim Simon as one of their own). However, bounded rationality is often modelled within the literature as the addition of further constraints on a utility-maximisation process. It is not at all clear how this should be categorised according to the framework of Earl (2005). On one hand, it attempts to take account of psychological constraints in economic decision-making and so in that sense can be viewed as an extension of psychological principles into the economics domain, placing it securely within the field of psychological economics along with behavioural economics. However, on the other hand, by maintaining the neoclassical assumption of utility-maximising agents, it extends economic methodology into decision-making situations that are traditionally the domain of psychologists, locating it within the economic psychology field.

The distinction

Behavioural economics, then, is the study of all aspects of economic decision-making. This includes the nature of people's preferences, both personal and pro-social; the actual cognitive processes that decision-makers employ when making their decisions; and the ways in which such decision-making is influenced by wider factors and so can be manipulated (both in positive and negative ways for decision-makers). Bounded rationality, by contrast, is much more narrowly focused on the analysis of decision-making when the decision-maker does not possess the cognitive capacity required to make a decision in the globally optimal manner because of its complexity. In terms of their focuses of study, then, works of bounded rationality form a subset within the field of behavioural economics; but in terms of their methodologies, works of bounded rationality often adopt the economic psychology approach, whereas those of behavioural economics adopt that of psychological economics.

Overview

In order to address the four issues outlined above, this research monograph proceeds in the following way.

Chapter 2

This is a survey of the recent developments within the behavioural economics literature. Given the size of this literature (alluded to above), this survey is particularly focused on the relevant articles identified by a recent online literature search, the majority of which were published between 2007 and 2015; and it seeks to be representative of the literature rather than fully comprehensive. In order to structure the literature in a meaningful way, the works of which it is composed are divided into the following four categories according to their nature, which are then subdivided further:

1   *Behavioural traits*: works that seek to shed further light on the nature and processes of human decision-making.

2   *Survey*: works that examine the literature itself, either in terms of its historical development, a particular theme within it, or the ways in which it can be used to shed light on other fields of economics.

3   *Application*: works that are concerned with the wider implications (either theoretical or methodological) of findings within the behavioural economics literature.

4   *Overarching*: works that seek to address the fundamental criticism of behavioural economics: that it has identified a whole array of different behaviours in different situations, but it has not generated a corresponding framework as to which behaviour occurs in which situations, thereby leading to perceptions that behavioural economics rests on arbitrary and *ad hoc* assumptions.

Chapter 3

Mirroring the structure for the behavioural economics literature review, this is a survey of the bounded rationality literature, in which the focus is also on recent developments in particular, drawing on the results from the same online literature search. It is immediately evident that the bounded rationality literature is less diverse than that of behavioural economics, with the taxonomy consisting of only *investigation* and *survey* works. The definitions of these are necessarily different to those employed in Chapter 2. Works of investigation primarily seek to examine the wider economic effects of decision-makers being cognitively unable to make their decisions as if in accordance with the standard model of rational choice. These works are subdivided according to the nature of the decision situation; namely, those of *standard choice* (choice among options that bring immediate payoffs); *uncertain choice* (choice among options that bring payoffs that are not fully understood by the decision-maker); *inter-temporal choice* (choice among options that bring future payoffs); *strategic choice* (choice among options that depend crucially on the decisions expected of others); and *macroeconomic behaviour* (behavioural choices that affect the wider macroeconomy). The survey papers identified in the bounded rationality literature critically examine either the literature as a whole according to particular criteria or more specific facets of the field and the lessons that have been learned from them (particularly the former).

Chapter 4

In this chapter the two literatures are examined and compared empirically. The intention of the analysis presented is to identify the audiences of works of behavioural economics and bounded rationality, and the academic standing that these works have within the economics discipline. Both of these questions are examined with reference to the academic journals (within economics) in which these works are published. The final intention is to examine the breadth of the impact that these works have through an econometric (linear regression) analysis of the number of citations that these works have accrued. This analysis demonstrates that the greatest proportion of bounded rationality articles are published in the highest ranking journals (according to the ranking produced by the *Association of Business Schools*), whereas the greatest proportion of behavioural economics articles are published in journals of the second highest ranking. Furthermore, articles of bounded rationality tend to be published in the more general, theoretical journals, which is perhaps unsurprising given the nature of the bounded rationality approach. However, there is no significant difference in the impact of bounded rationality and behavioural economics articles when relevant factors have been controlled.

Chapter 5

Building on the findings from the previous three chapters, in this chapter the two literatures are compared according to a number of characteristics: their focuses, methodological approaches, research methods, fields of application and analytical power. This chapter demonstrates that the two literatures have indeed evolved along different paths, but that they complement each other, together enhancing our understanding of economic decision-making and its wider economic effects. This chapter concludes with a discussion about the criticisms to which the two approaches have been subjected and how these could be addressed by bringing them closer together: especially regarding the fundamental criticism of behavioural economics mentioned above.

Chapter 6

In this penultimate chapter, a new approach is outlined to address the fundamental criticism levelled against behavioural economics, which is based on viewing decision-making as a two-step procedure. In the first step (the 'higher-order' decision), the decision-maker chooses how much of his limited cognitive resource (based on the ever-growing findings regarding decision fatigue) to allocate to a particular decision. This then determines the degree to which the particular decision (the second step, 'lower-order' decision) can be made as if according to utility maximisation (conversely, the degree to which it is made through satisficing). In this approach, then, the focus is on the degree of optimisation with which a decision is made rather than the precise choice that is taken (an avenue that has not yet been explored in the literature), and behaviour is rationalised at the higher-order level of cognitive resource allocation. A model along these lines is sketched, reformulating the Hicks and Allen (1934) theory of value as an example of such lower-order decision-making: a reformulation that generates propositions that are empirically supported.

Chapter 7

A concluding discussion is presented in this final chapter, summarising the findings of this monograph in relation to the four issues outlined at the start of this introduction. The disciplines of behavioural economics and bounded rationality are both exceptionally fruitful: according to their contributions to our understanding of economic decision-making; their contributions to economic policy-making; and the ways in which they have raised the profile of the subject as a whole. Countering the pressures that are causing them to evolve along such different paths, and so bringing them closer together in collaboration, could be the key to releasing the next surge of findings, particularly with regards to addressing the criticisms that have been levelled against them.

References

Avineri, E. (2012) 'On the use and potential of behavioural economics from the perspective of transport and climate change', *Journal of Transport Geography* 24, 512–521.

Burnham, T.C. (2013) 'Towards a neo-Darwinian synthesis of neoclassical and behavioral economics', *Journal of Economic Behavior and Organization* 90S, S113–S127.

Camerer, C.F. (2007) 'Neuroeconomics: using neuroscience to make economic predictions', *Economic Journal* 117, C26–C42.

Earl, P.E. (2005) 'Economics and psychology in the twenty-first century', *Cambridge Journal of Economics* 29, 909–926.

Fetchenhauer, D., Azar, O.H., Antonides, G., Dunning, D., Frank, R.H., Lea, S. and Örlander, F. (2012) 'Monozygotic twins or unrelated stepchildren? On the relationship between economic psychology and behavioral economics', *Journal of Economic Psychology* 33, 695–699.

Frantz, R. (2004) 'The behavioral economics of George Akerlof and Harvey Leibenstein', *Journal of Socio-Economics* 33, 29–44.

Heiner, R.A. (1983) 'The origin of predictable behavior', *American Economic Review* 73, 560–595.

Hicks, J.R. and Allen, R.G.D. (1934) 'A reconsideration of the theory of value, part 1', *Economica* 1, 52–76.

Kahneman, D. and Tversky, A. (1979) 'Prospect theory: an analysis of decision under risk', *Econometrica* 47, 263–291.

Nobelprize.org (2014) 'The Sveriges Riksbank Prize in Economic Sciences in Memory of Alfred Nobel 1978', Nobel Media AB 2014, accessed 15 December 2014, www.nobelprize.org/nobel_prizes/economic-sciences/laureates/1978/.

Robbins, L. (1932) *An Essay on the Nature and Significance of Economic Science*, London: Macmillan.

Rogers, B.W., T.R. Palfrey and C.F. Camerer (2009) 'Heterogeneous quantal response equilibrium and cognitive hierarchies', *Journal of Economic Theory* 144, 1440–1467.

Rubinstein, A. (2007) 'Instinctive and cognitive reasoning: a study of response times', *Economic Journal* 117, 1243–1259.

Sargent, T.J. (1993) *Bounded Rationality in Macroeconomics*, Oxford: Oxford University Press.

Sent, E.-M. (1997) 'Sargent versus Simon: bounded rationality unbound', *Cambridge Journal of Economics* 21, 323–339.

Simon, H.A. (1955) 'A behavioural model of rational choice', *Quarterly Journal of Economics* 69, 99–118.

Simon, H.A. (1957) *Models of man: social and rational*, New York and London: John Wiley.

Simon, H.A. (1991) *Models of My Life*, New York: Basic Books.

Simon, H.A., Egidi, M., Viale, R. and Marris, R. (1992) *Economics, Bounded Rationality and the Cognitive Revolution*, Cheltenham, UK: Edward Elgar Publishing Limited.

Tversky, A. and Kahneman, D. (1974) 'Judgment under uncertainty: heuristics and biases', *Science* 185, 1124–1130.

Uchitelle, L. (2001) 'Following the money, but also the mind: some economists call behavior a key', *New York Times*, 11 February, Section 3.

2 Recent developments in the behavioural economics literature

A survey

The behavioural economics literature has expanded at an astonishing rate over the past few decades, and it continues to do so. Indeed, according to Burnham (2013) there is now in excess of 50,000 papers citing the works of Kahneman and Tversky (1979) and Tversky and Kahneman (1974). The literature has also been extended in a whole array of different directions in terms of its fields of study but also the purposes of its works. As such, the objective of this chapter is to present a taxonomy by which this literature can be structured and analysed, to identify and provide a reflective overview of each of the main themes and components of which it is composed. Given its size, though, the intention is for this survey to be representative of the literature rather than for it to be wholly comprehensive. With this in mind, the survey that follows focuses in particular on recent developments within the literature by primarily examining the relevant articles identified in an online literature search using the *EBSCOhost Online Research Database*, examining each journal in the *Association of Business Schools Academic Journal Quality Guide* (version 4 – see Harvey *et al.*, 2010) in turn, using 'behavioural economics' as the designated subject term. These articles, generally published between 2007 and 2015, are outlined in Appendix 2.1.

The general taxonomy that is to be used in this exploration of the behavioural economics literature is presented in Figure 2.1. In order to clarify the structure of the literature, each of these higher-level categories is subdivided in the sections that follow.

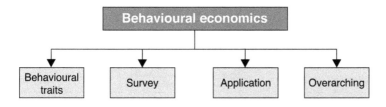

Figure 2.1 Behavioural economics: a general taxonomy

Behavioural traits

The behavioural traits component of the literature consists of works that seek to shed further light on the nature and processes of human decision-making. This is by far the largest element of the literature being reviewed here and so it is subdivided further into six lower-level categories in order that the nature of its constituent works, and the linkages between them, can be most easily identified. This sub-taxonomy is presented in Figure 2.2 and each category is examined in turn below.

Investigation

A body of work within the behavioural economics literature is concerned with the higher-level question that asks how the nature and processes of human decision-making can be examined. A number of these papers examine how preferences can be elicited. Dickhaut *et al.* (2013a), for example, demonstrate that preferences in high-stake situations can be induced, and so examined, in a low-stake environment, making the investigation of such preferences easier. In a related paper, Harrison *et al.* (2013) reduce to its fundamental elements the experimental binary lottery procedure for inducing risk-neutral behaviour in order to evaluate it as a method for eliciting such preferences. The authors find that the procedure induces a statistically significant shift toward risk neutrality: a result that is also true when subjects make several lottery choices, from which one is selected for payment. Takanori and Goto (2009) present a method for measuring time and risk preferences simultaneously, using stated preference discrete choice model analysis, which they then apply to an investigation of smoking behaviour using a survey dataset of Japanese smokers. As final examples of such papers, Weber (2012) presents a Becker-DeGroot-Marshak mechanism that is adjusted to take account of the person's income compensation, asserting that it can generate testable hypotheses for the income-compensated endowment effect as a behavioral anomaly; while Alevy *et al.* (2011) find that people's preferences are inconsistently expressed across the joint and isolated methods of valuation (valuing two or more goods together and valuing a single good in isolation, respectively) for both public and private goods, and that this effect is accentuated when there is uncertainty about the quality of the good but reduced with the experience of the respondent.

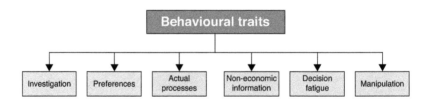

Figure 2.2 Behavioural economics: the behavioural traits literature

Other papers in this stream examine the use of direct feedback from subjects. For instance, Branas-Garza *et al.* (2011) examine the extent to which self-reports from subjects effectively explain their behaviour in a traveller's dilemma game. In this particular case, the authors find that an array of factors lie beneath the observed behaviour, including the subjects' aspiration levels, competitive behaviour and attitudes towards risk. They also find that a subject's self-justification is coherent with his behaviour in other tests and experiments, including how much they give in an experiment of a dictator game and their choices when facing uncertainty in two different tasks; and so conclude that such feedback is informative about a subject's general behaviour. Fenichel *et al.* (2009), by contrast, examine the effects of including 'no opinion' response options in choice questionnaires. Using a split-sample design, the authors find that including more than one of these response options may enable researchers to differentiate between respondents who choose no-opinion options due to satisficing and those expressing utility indifference; and that treating them as negative responses can alter substantially the resulting preference estimates.

Preferences

The most substantial component of the literature seeking to uncover new insights into actual decision-making is that concerned with the nature of human preferences: personal preferences regarding present choices and the future, and also pro-social preferences.

In the first of these categories, for example, Fehr-Duda *et al.* (2011) examine the determinants of the weights that people put on small and large probabilities when they are valuing risky prospects. The authors find that feelings may have an effect on such decision-making, thereby making risk preferences potentially susceptible to factors irrelevant to the decision at hand. In a similar vein, Barham *et al.* (2014) test for the effects of risk and ambiguity aversion on the adoption of genetic modification technology (risk being defined as a negative effect with a known probability distribution and ambiguity as a negative effect for which the probability distribution is uncertain), finding that ambiguity aversion increases the pace of such technological adoption: a finding that is in contrast to other studies within the literature. Tonin and Vlassopoulos (2013), by contrast, contribute to a growing literature concerned with the effects of self-image on economic behaviour, concluding from the play of a dictator game in which players are able to alter their choices in a second stage, that initial choices are influenced by self-image concerns but that once players have signalled their good natures they are more readily self-serving. Related to this is the work of Lightle (2013) into two variants of a sender-receiver game in which the meaning of the communicated message is unclear, demonstrating that as players gain experience, they tell stronger and more frequent lies, suggesting that lie aversion is not a standard characteristic of communication in noisy situations. Finally, Gherzi *et al.* (2014) find that investors actively seek more information about their investments following the receipt of both positive and negative news (what the authors term the 'meerkat effect'): a finding that runs counter to other works in the literature, which demonstrate that people seek less information following receipt of negative news (the 'ostrich effect', coined by Galai and Sade, 2006, and supported by Loewenstein *et al.*, 2003; Karlsson *et al.*, 2009; and Sicherman *et al.*, 2013).

Other papers in the literature examine the origins of people's preferences. For instance, Cesarini *et al.* (2009) compare monozygotic twins (who share the same set of genes) to dizygotic twins (who possess different genes) in order to estimate the proportion of observed behavioural differences that is hereditary and the proportions that are due to being in common and individual environments: the nature versus nurture question. The authors find evidence that preferences for risk taking and giving are inherited. In related papers, Oreopoulos and Salvanes (2011) examine the nonmonetary effects of schooling, including how it affects both people's preferences and their decisions in life; Hyll and Schneider (2013) examine whether or not TV consumption has an impact on material aspirations, concluding that watching TV is positively correlated with aspirations and that the relationship is causal; and Van Hoorn and Maseland (2013) find strong support for the existence of a Protestant work ethic, demonstrating that individual Protestants and societies that are historically Protestant both appear to value work significantly more, and that the effect of living in a Protestant society dominates the effect of actually being Protestant.

In the second category of investigations into the nature of preferences (specifically addressing personal preferences about the future) is the work of Brown *et al.* (2009), which tests two explanations for why people save less than the standard optimal amounts: the first being that they are boundedly rational and so cognitively unable to ascertain the optimal amounts; and the second being that they possess a preference for immediate consumption. The authors find that people quickly learn to save the optimal amounts, thereby eliminating the explanation of bounded rationality, and that they exhibit a present-bias, which is consistent with both the theory of hyperbolic discounting and also the dual-self model. In a related study, Finke and Huston (2013) find that the importance subjects place on saving for retirement is more effectively predicted by a combination of different intertemporal behaviour (especially by behaviour regarding preventative health measures) than by a measure of time preference that involves subjects comparing dollar amounts across time. Also within this category, Sloan *et al.* (2014) examine the behavioural characteristics of drink-drivers compared to other drinkers, concluding that the former are relatively knowledgeable about the relevant legislation but that they are more impulsive and exhibit hyperbolic discounting more than other drinkers.

The third category consists of works that examine pro-social preferences, the most studied of which is the preference to cooperate with others. Vanberg (2008), for example, examines why pre-play commitments lead to greater cooperation between subjects in experimental games. The author concludes that, from the two possible explanations that have been proposed in the literature, this effect is best explained by people possessing a preference for keeping their word (proposed by Ellingsen and Johannesson, 2004) rather than them wanting to avoid the guilt associated with letting other people down (Dufwenberg and Gneezy, 2000; Charness and Dufwenberg, 2006; Battigalli and Dufwenberg, 2007;). Related to this work are the papers of Volk *et al.* (2012), D'Exelle and van den Berg (2014), Bigoni *et al.* (2013) and Pirinsky (2013). In the first of these, the authors find that preferences for cooperation are remarkably stable at the aggregate level and, to a lesser degree, at the individual level; and that, from among a list of standard personality traits, cooperation is most closely associated with that of 'agree-ableness'. The authors of the second paper find from an experimental study of aid distribution and cooperation in a field lab in rural Nicaragua that the presence of a representative member in a group alters the total contributions made by group members. In the third, the authors find substantial differences between the behaviour of students and clerical workers, and also between the behaviour exhibited when there is the facility to personally punish another player and when this is not a possibility. With regards to preferences for cooperation, they find that students exhibit higher levels of aggregate cooperation than clerical workers and that students are less likely than clerical workers to adopt unconditional strategies (they also find that students are more inclined to punish defections by others). In the final of these four examples, Pirinsky (2013) examines data from the *World Values Survey* and finds that, among other things, more confident individuals participate in more social networks and are more actively involved in cooperation, although the economic impact of confidence varies significantly across cultures. In contrast to these works, in a study of sender-receiver games, Sheremeta and Shields (2013) find that the majority of players adopt deceptive strategies (sending favourable messages when the true state of the game is unfavourable) when acting as the sender, and that the honest behaviour of some senders can be explained by pro-social preferences.

Other contributions to this part of the literature examine feelings of unfairness. For example, Cornelissen *et al.* (2013) present evidence from the *German Socio-Economic Panel* dataset that feelings of unfairness about the taxation system, in the sense that the rich (more specifically their employers) are not paying enough tax, can lead to a 20 per cent rise in absenteeism from work. Bjornskov *et al.* (2013) demonstrate that there exist a negative association between perceptions that the income generation process is fair and the demand for more equal incomes, and a positive association between such fairness perceptions and subjective wellbeing. Zubrickas (2012) demonstrates theoretically that experience of markets can support the evolution of such pro-social preferences, showing that a member of a group is incentivised to distribute the group's endowment equally in order to minimise the severity of any abuse of market power to which the group is subjected.

Actual processes

The papers in this category address the actual processes and biases involved in decision-making. Beshears and Milkman (2011), for example, present evidence of the 'escalation bias' (the behavioural trait that people increase their commitment to a particular stance after it has been shown to be incorrect) in the behaviour of financial analysts when forecasting a company's quarterly earnings, even though such behaviour reduces forecasting accuracy and is not financially incentivised. Ivanov *et al.* (2013) find that behaviour observed from a herding game is, among other things, characterised by an excessive reluctance to invest in response to market activity (the 'conservatism bias'). The papers of McAlvanah and Moul (2013), Bucchianeri and Minson (2013) and Corrigan *et al.* (2014) all present evidence of anchoring effects in behaviour. In the first of these, the authors find that Australian bookmakers exhibit anchoring on the original odds offered, failing to fully readjust the odds in response to a horse being withdrawn from the race at the last minute and consequently earning 20 per cent less. In the second, the authors analyse more than 14,000 residential property sales and find that, *ceteris paribus*, higher initial listing prices are associated with higher eventual selling prices: for the average home in their sample, over-pricing between 10 per cent and 20 per cent leads to an increase in the sale price of US\$117–163 (suggesting that traders anchor on initial listing prices). And in the third of these papers, the authors find a positive correlation between bids made during practice rounds of an experimental auction and the actual bids that are subsequently made. Other papers, such as those of Oechssler *et al.* (2009) and Alos-Ferrer and Hugelschafer (2012), examine the determinants of such behavioural biases. The first of these finds that incidences of most biases are lower among people with higher cognitive abilities (based on the *cognitive reflection test* of Frederick, 2005) but they still remain substantial; while the second finds that greater faith in intuition is associated with an increased use of the representativeness heuristic (the overweighting of sample information) but not with increased conservatism (the overweighting of prior information), and that subjects with greater faith in intuition tend to repeat successful decisions even if correctly updating their beliefs would lead to alternative behaviour (the 'reinforcement heuristic'). Miravete and Palacios-Huerta (2014), however, present empirical evidence that consumers do not make permanent mistakes and that any inertia in consumption is most likely caused by 'rational inattention' as consumers are active in searching for the best deals.

Other papers in the literature examine the more general processes involved in decision-making. Rubinstein (2007), for instance, examines the response times of students answering game theory problems online and suggests that there are three such responses, which he labels *cognitive* (actions that involve a reasoning process), *instinctive* (actions that involve instinct) and *reasonless* (actions that are likely to be the outcome of a random process). Dickhaut *et al.* (2013b), by contrast, present a stylised model of the brain processes engaged in evaluating information, which they demonstrate generates several features of decision-making that are consistent with experimental evidence. Lindner and Sutter (2013), employing the '11–20 money request game' of Arad and Rubinstein (2012), find that the depth of people's reasoning is limited, even after repetitions of the game (suggesting limited learning), but that behaviour is closer to that of the standard equilibrium when subjects are exposed to time pressure, which they suggest evokes intuitive reasoning (or instinctive decision-making in the categories of Rubinstein, 2007, above).

Non-economic information

These papers are concerned with the way in which final decisions are affected by the manner in which the possible options are presented to decision-makers: framing effects. Kallbekken *et al.* (2011), for example, demonstrate that framing environmental policies as 'taxes' reduces the support for them, whereas hypothecating the revenues they raise can increase support. List and Samek (2015) and McCluskey *et al.* (2011) examine how framing effects can be employed to 'nudge' children to eat more healthily. List and Samek (2015) find that the way in which incentives (which are effective) are framed (whether as gains or losses) has little effect on consumption choices, although combining an educational message with a loss-framed incentive causes a longer-lasting increase in the consumption of healthy snacks. McCluskey *et al.* (2011), however, find that altering menus to include a range of options, including healthier items, rather than having an unhealthy default option that comes with every meal, causes sales of unhealthy options to decline. Both of these studies find evidence of learning over time: the first arising from educational messages and the second from marketing. In related papers, Di Guida *et al.* (2012) find that the basic properties of decisions from experience are not significantly altered by options to rely on defaults that are determined by the decision-makers themselves, but that the introduction of default options reduces the status quo bias; Chandler and Kapelner (2013) find that, *ceteris paribus*, employees produce a greater quantity of output when informed that their work is meaningful (in this particular study, that they were labelling tumor cells in order to assist medical researchers) and that those informed that their work is meaningless (in this case, that their work would be discarded) produce a lower quality of output (with no change in quantity); and Riener and Wiederhold (2013) find that the same method of inducting members into a group can lead to significantly different subsequent behaviour of the members, which they explain is determined by the quality of the relationship established between the group members and which they assert has important implications for the design of experimental studies.

Decision fatigue

The study of the nature and effects of decision fatigue (the notion that decision-makers possess finite cognitive resources that are consumed during acts of volition, such as decision-making and exerting self-control) is an expanding part of the literature. Bucciol *et al.* (2011), for instance, examine the effect of decision fatigue on economic productivity. More specifically, they examine the effect of exposing children between the ages of six and thirteen to the temptation of an unhealthy snack on their subsequent productivity. They find that, exposing younger children to the 'marshmallow test' (showing them a snack but instructing them that they are not allowed to eat it while the experimenter is absent) causes their subsequent productivity to significantly decline, whereas the same temptation has little effect on the subsequent productivity of older children. Arunachalam *et al.* (2009) test for the related 'excessive-choice effect' (that when the number of options from which consumers can choose is increased, the total amount of consumption falls), finding that some subjects actually state a preference for facing fewer options and that there is evidence of the effect, but that the evidence is weaker than that in the literature. Cadena and Keys (2013) present evidence that the reason why one in six undergraduate students choose to turn down the offer of interest-free loans (in effect, turning down a substantial free gift of money from the government) lies in the desire of students to avoid the increased temptation that having such extra liquidity would bring in the future: a possibly rational response to the fear of future decision fatigue.

Manipulation

A number of works in the literature examine whether or not people's preferences can be altered by government interventions. For example, Kits *et al.* (2014) study motivational crowding out (the observation that material incentives can erode self-motivation) in the case of environmental conservation auctions (programmes whereby landowners bid competitively for grants to fund environmentally friendly practices, with the strongest bids being awarded the contracts). The authors find that the introduction and subsequent removal of such an auction significantly reduces voluntary action to improve environmental quality compared to the situation in which an auction never exists. This is in contrast to that of Bengtsson and Engstrom (2013), which demonstrates that replacing traditional trust-based contracts with an increased level of monitoring (in this case by the Swedish foreign aid agency on Swedish non-profit organisations) does not affect participation but does improve efficiency. Stahl (2013) finds that a Kandori reputation-labelling mechanism (which Kandori, 1992, demonstrated is sufficient to support cooperation in a prisoners' dilemma game) increases the level of cooperation with experience; whereas Hoffman *et al.* (2013) find that exaggerating the contributions of all other players in a public goods game by 25 per cent fails to significantly increase the contributions of others in the short-term and, when the manipulation is revealed, serves to reduce the contributions in the long-term; but that exaggerating contributions in a case-by-case fashion, ensuring that no player is informed of having contributed more than the average, causes contributions to stabilise at very high levels in both the short term and after the manipulation is revealed. In a final related paper, McAlvanah (2010) examines the effects caused to a person's utility function and inter-temporal discount function by dividing time into intervals. The author demonstrates that such subdivision of time causes individuals to display increased relative impatience for negative amounts of money than for positive amounts of money, and that these effects are stronger when delaying an early gain (or hastening a later loss) than for hastening a later gain (or delaying an earlier loss).

Survey

A sizeable part of the behavioural economics literature is composed of survey articles, which can be disaggregated into three further categories: developmental, analytical and suggestive surveys – as illustrated in Figure 2.3.

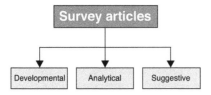

Figure 2.3 Survey articles in behavioural economics

Developmental surveys

The first of these sub-categories, the developmental surveys, consists of works concerned with tracing and examining the historical or thematic development of behavioural economics as a field of study. For example, Ashraf *et al.* (2005) outline the psychological elements of Adam Smith's *The Theory of Moral Sentiments* and their connections with modern behavioural economics, suggesting in particular that Smith's work is very similar to the dual-self models of behavioural economics (see, for example, Bernheim and Rangel, 2004) and that it pre-empts findings about loss aversion, willpower and fairness. In Campbell (2014), the contributions of Eugene Fama, Lars Peter Hansen and Robert Shiller are surveyed, and the relationships between them explored, in the field of empirical asset pricing, in which a section is devoted to their works relating to behavioural economics and finance. Taking more specific focuses, Di Clemente and Hantula (2003) analyse the development of behavioural economics in the field of consumer theory, which in the 1970s widened into addressing environmental issues such as recycling and energy conservation; Earl (2011) examines the significant use of anecdotes, as illustrative evidence of findings and as the motivation for research, in the development and growth of behavioural economics; Augier and March (2008) examine the trade-off between behavioural realism and model simplicity in behavioural economics through an assessment of the works of, and the correspondence between, Herbert Simon and Oliver Williamson; and Frantz (2004) examines the works of George Akerlof and Harvey Leibenstein, asserting that they make significant contributions to the wider development of behavioural economics.

Analytical surveys

Analytical survey articles critically examine either the behavioural economics literature as a whole according to particular criteria or more specific facets of the field and the lessons that have been learned from them. Taking the first of these approaches, for example, Crawford (2013) outlines two approaches to modelling decision-making within the behavioural economics literature: bounded rationality models that do not assume optimisation but continue to make standard assumptions about preferences; and optimisation-based behavioural models that continue to assume optimisation but relax standard assumptions about the nature of preferences.

The author supports the view of Rabin (2013a), disagreeing with that of Harstad and Selten (2013), that there should be a continued focus on the latter approach. Similarly, Charness *et al.* (2013a) survey the types of experiments employed in behavioural economics. In addition to the typical laboratory and field experiment distinction, the authors suggest there should be a category of 'extra-laboratory' experiments, which are essentially conducted in the same manner as laboratory experiments but not on a university campus and not with the standard student population. Dellavigna (2009) presents a survey of the empirical findings in behavioural economics as a whole, covering all aspects of decision-making.

Barberis (2013a) adopts the second, more specific, focus, surveying the developments in our understanding of tail events (which are defined as 'rare, high-impact events': 611), which primarily concerns the probability weighting used in judgements about such events. Also more specifically focused are the surveys of Gul and Pesendorfer (2007), of the role of welfare economics in the face of the findings in behavioural economics; Gundersen *et al.* (2012), of recent investigations into the behavioural economics of obesity; Dohmen (2014), of the behavioural labour economics literature and of the impact that behavioural economics has had on the field of labour economics more widely; Kliger *et al.* (2014), of 25 articles that were accepted into the special issue of the *Journal of Economic Behavior & Organization* on empirical behavioural finance, with an emphasis on innovative empirical methods; Jantti *et al.* (2014a), of the articles in the special issue of the *Review of Income & Wealth* on development and behavioural economics; Charness *et al.* (2013b), of the experimental methods used in the literature to elicit people's preferences regarding risk; Stringham (2011), of the literature addressing the role of personal moral constraints on economic behaviour; Barberis (2013b), of the development and use of prospect theory in economics as a whole; and Shiller (2014), of the role of behavioural factors in the determination of asset prices.

Suggestive surveys

Survey articles of the suggestive type are those that suggest how the findings of behavioural economics relate to other particular fields or issues in economics, to which it has not yet been turned. The feature that distinguishes these articles from the analytical surveys above is the *status* of the research in the particular field. Analytical surveys are concerned with examining the findings of research that has already been conducted in the particular field, or to do with the particular issue at hand; whereas the articles here are concerned with ways in which existing work applies to fields and issues that have not yet been specifically researched. Similarly, the distinguishing feature between these articles and those in the higher-level application category below is the *nature* of the research. The suggestive survey papers here do not present original findings about economic behaviour: they take existing findings from the behavioural economics literature and examine how they can be applied to new fields or discussions. In essence, they either outline a programme of future research or they present a new, behavioural explanation for existing phenomena.

Adopting the first of these approaches, and so outlining programmes of future research, are the surveys of Gowdy (2008), Brekke and Johansson-Stenman (2008), Avineri (2012) and Datta and Mullainathan (2014). In the first and second of these, the authors survey the behavioural economics literature to draw out lessons about the economics of climate change, with the first paper focusing in particular on the implications for policy and the second focusing on the implications of prospect theory, decision fatigue and the way that an individual's discount rate alters over time for the choice of the social discount rate, and also on the implications of the experimental findings relating to cooperation, reciprocal behaviour and social norms for climate change negotiations. The third of these examples presents a related survey, which examines how findings in behavioural economics can contribute to travel demand modelling and the design of policies to change transport behaviour in order to reduce its climate change effects. The last of these examples presents a survey of how the behavioural economics literature can inform the design and implementation of development policies.

Adopting the second approach, and so surveying the behavioural economics literature in order to provide a new explanation for existing phenomena, are the surveys of Astebro *et al.* (2014), Benartzi *et al.* (2011), D'Orlando and Ferrante (2009) and De Coninck (2011). The first of these presents an explanation for the puzzle as to why entrepreneurs enter and persist with entrepreneurship despite the expectation of low risk-adjusted returns; an explanation that is based on notions of risk aversion, overconfidence and the taste for non-pecuniary benefits (although the authors concede that no single factor can be taken as a satisfactory explanation in isolation). The second presents an explanation for the puzzle as to why people choose to buy so few annuities when they come to retirement; the third an explanation of the different types of labour market regulations used in different countries, which is based on differences in the extent to which labour-force behaviour is characterised by certain biases and heuristics; and the fourth assesses whether findings in behavioural economics, such as the endowment effect, can be used to explain the general lack of empirical support for the findings in comparative law. In a completely different style of paper, Crettez and Deloche (2013) make use of experimental evidence to compare the last two versions of Molière's *Tartuffe*, interpreting the final version of the play (there were three) as consisting of two stag hunt games, one without pre-game communication and one with; and interpreting the penultimate version of the play as also involving pre-game communication in the first stag hunt game, but with the players failing to reach the efficient equilibrium. The authors suggest that, by removing the pre-game communication from the first game, Molière adapted his play as if he had been a student of modern behavioural game theory.

Application

Articles in this category are concerned with the wider implications of findings within the behavioural economics literature. They tend to fall into two groups. The first are those works that embed behavioural findings into theoretical models in order to examine the wider, theoretical effects of increased behavioural realism in given situations. The second are those works that examine how behavioural findings affect the economist's toolkit: the techniques of analysis in economics.

The paper by Wrede (2011) sits in the first of these groups. In this work, the author integrates hyperbolic discounting into a three-period model of child-bearing, which leads the author to conclude that without the opportunity to shift the financial burden of rearing children into the future, hyperbolic discounters will give birth to fewer children; but that with the opportunity to do this, the impact of hyperbolic discounting on births depends on the underlying motive for motherhood. A similar approach is also adopted in Kanbur *et al.* (2008), which integrates behavioural findings arising from prospect theory into a model of optimal income taxation, which causes the standard results of the latter in situations of uncertainty to be in need of modification. Other papers in this group include those of Hadjiyiannis *et al.* (2012), Aronsson and Granlund (2011), Fudenberg and Levine (2012), De Clippel (2014), Evren (2012) and Sorger and Stark (2013), each of which is briefly examined in turn. Hadjiyiannis *et al.* (2012) develop a model of international trade agreements in which they embed the effects of both perceptions of fairness and reciprocity; finding, among other things, that reciprocal countries that are moderately demanding of their trading partners regarding their trade policies can support a greater degree of cooperation than self-interested ones, but that when only very liberal trade policies are considered fair, then reciprocity could have a detrimental effect on cooperation. Aronsson and Granlund (2011) theoretically examine the effect of present-biased consumers on the government provision of a public good. Fudenberg and Levine (2012) further develop the dual-self model of self-control by including a cognitive resource variable (a stock of willpower) that takes into account the cost of the self-control that has been exerted in the past, which they use to examine when consumption decisions will be avoided and delayed. De Clippel (2014) examines implementation theory (which is concerned with the integration of a mechanism into a game such that the outcome of a game conforms to a given criterion of optimality) to situations in which subjects possess complete information but are not rational, extending the result of Maskin (1999) of Nash implementability. Evren (2012) addresses the puzzle as to why people choose to vote in large electorates, presenting a model that successfully explains the puzzle in which some voters are altruistic towards others but in which the proportion of altruistic voters is uncertain among the supporters of a given candidate. And in the final example, Sorger and Stark (2013) present a model demonstrating that a rank-preserving redistribution of income from rich to poor (a *Pigou-Dalton transfer*) can actually exacerbate income inequality, because the poor may respond to the reduced feelings of relative deprivation by reducing their work effort.

In the second group are the works of Gunther and Maier (2014) and Jantti *et al.* (2014b). In the first of these, the authors examine how findings from behavioural economics (particularly those on reference-dependent utility) affect measures of (perceived) multi-period poverty and vulnerability, in particular making poverty a function of both expected consumption levels and also expected losses and gains in consumption. In the second, the authors examine the measurement of social welfare, poverty and inequality in the light of behavioural findings arising from prospect theory (in particular, reference dependence, loss aversion and diminishing sensitivity), which leads them to propose a new notion of 'equivalent income' as the basis of measuring poverty and inequality.

Overarching

The behavioural economics literature is increasingly concerned to address the fundamental criticism of the field: that it has identified a whole array of different behaviour in different situations but it has not generated a corresponding framework as to which behaviour occurs in which situations, thereby leading to perceptions that behavioural economics rests on arbitrary and *ad hoc* assumptions. As Spiegler (2011: 200) comments:

> What mutes the ad-hockery criticism in the case of the rational-choice model is the existence of a coherent analytical framework, in which all standard economic models are embedded. A comparable abstract framework is, in my opinion, what is missing the most from the current bounded rationality and behavioral economics literature.

The works in this category are concerned with the development of such overarching theories for behavioural economics, which can provide a feasible alternative to the neoclassical framework.

One such work is that of Rabin (2013b), which suggests the direction in which such modelling should go. More specifically, Rabin argues that 'more of our efforts to improve the psychological realism of economics should be devoted to developing (necessarily imperfect) portable, mathematical models' (617), or 'portable extensions of existing models [PEEMS]' (618), which have two key characteristics. First, they embed new parameters into existing models so that the new psychological assumptions are represented as parameter values that are clearly different to those of the standard model of rational choice. Second, they are defined across economics using the same independent variables as those used in existing research, thereby making it applicable across the subject.

The model that has the greatest prominence in this regard is perhaps that of Bernheim and Rangel (2009), which is an alternative general choice framework that takes account of a wide array of non-rational behaviours observed and reported within behavioural economics. At its heart is the replacement of the standard revealed preference relation with an 'unambiguous choice relation', which in its strict sense is defined as good Y never being chosen if good X is available. Mandler (2014) examines the effectiveness of using the Pareto criterion to rank outcomes when people (or a single person in the case of the dual-self model) possess preferences of the type modelled in Bernheim and Rangel (2009). In models such as that of Bernheim and Rangel (2009), and also those of Salant and Rubinstein (2008) and Mandler (2004, 2005), the different versions of an individual (the different selves) who make their choices at different times disagree about how to rank outcomes X and Y, and so there is no complete behavioural welfare ranking of these outcomes for the individual as a whole. Mandler (2014) demonstrates that such incomplete welfare relations can cause the set of Pareto optima to be very large, thereby eliminating the Pareto criterion's capacity to rank allocations effectively. In related work, Bradford *et al.* (2010) extend the standard model of utility maximisation to incorporate the effect of adaptation (the process by which utility reverts back to its level before a change in prices, quantities or income as decision-makers become accustomed to the new situation in which they find themselves). The authors call this the 'adaptive global utility model'. Bommier *et al.* (2012), by contrast, take a different approach, deriving a result about risk (uncertainty) aversion that is based on weak assumptions about ordinal preferences and the ability to rank states of the world. In this way, they demonstrate that informative results can be generated without it being necessary to make specific assumptions about rationality. The authors then apply this result to savings behaviour, demonstrating that risk uncertainty leads to greater precautionary saving.

References

Alevy, J.E., List, J.A. and Adamowicz, W.L. (2011) 'How can behavioral economics inform nonmarket valuation? An example from the preference reversal literature', *Land Economics* 87, 365–381.

Alos-Ferrer, C. and Hugelschafer, S. (2012) 'Faith in intuition and behavioral biases', *Journal of Economic Behavior & Organization* 84, 182–192.

Arad, A. and Rubinstein, A. (2012) 'The 11–20 money request game: a level-k reasoning study', *American Economic Review* 102, 3561–3573.

Aronsson, T. and Granlund, D. (2011) 'Public goods and optimal paternalism under present-biased preferences', *Economics Letters* 113, 54–57.

Arunachalam, B., Henneberry, S.R., Lusk, J.L. and Norwood, F.B. (2009) 'An empirical investigation into the excessive-choice effect', *American Journal of Agricultural Economics* 91, 810–825.

Ashraf, N., Camerer, C.F. and Loewenstein, G. (2005) 'Adam Smith, behavioral economist', *Journal of Economic Perspectives* 19, 131–145.

Astebro, T., Herz, H., Nanda, R. and Weber, R.A. (2014) 'Seeking the roots of entrepreneurship: insights from behavioral economics', *Journal of Economic Perspectives* 28, 49–70.

Augier, M. and March, J.G. (2008) 'Realism and comprehension in economics: a footnote to an exchange between Oliver E. Williamson and Herbert A. Simon', *Journal of Economic Behavior & Organization* 66, 95–105.

Avineri, E. (2012) 'On the use and potential of behavioural economics from the perspective of transport and climate change', *Journal of Transport Geography* 24, 512–521.

Barberis, N.C. (2013a) 'The psychology of tail events: progress and challenges', *American Economic Review, Papers and Proceedings* 103, 611–616.

Barberis, N.C (2013b) 'Thirty years of prospect theory in economics: a review and assessment', *Journal of Economic Perspectives* 27, 173–196.

Barham, B.L., Chavas, J.-P., Fitz, D., Rios Salas, V. and Schechter, L. (2014) 'The roles of risk and ambiguity in technology adoption', *Journal of Economic Behavior & Organization* 97, 204–218.

Battigalli, P. and Dufwenberg, M. (2007) 'Guilt in game', *American Economic Review, Papers and Proceedings* 97, 170–176.

Benartzi, S., Previtero, A. and Thaler, R.H. (2011) 'Annuitization puzzles', *Journal of Economic Perspectives* 25, 143–164.

Bengtsson, N. and Engstrom, P. (2013) 'Replacing trust with control: a field test of motivation crowd out theory', *Economic Journal* 124, 833–858.

Bernheim, D. and Rangel, A. (2004) 'Addiction and cue-triggered decision processes', *American Economic Review* 94, 1558–1590.

Bernheim, D. and Rangel A. (2009) 'Beyond revealed preference: choice-theoretic foundations for behavioral welfare economics', *Quarterly Journal of Economics* 124, 51–105.

Beshears, J. and Milkman, K.L. (2011) 'Do sell-side stock analysts exhibit escalation of commitment?', *Journal of Economic Behavior & Organization* 77, 304–317.

Bigoni, M., Camera, G. and Casari, M. (2013) 'Strategies of cooperation and punishment among students and clerical workers', *Journal of Economic Behavior & Organization* 94, 172–182.

Bjornskov, C., Dreher, A., Fischer, J.A.V., Schnellenbach, J. and Gehring, K. (2013) 'Inequality and happiness: when perceived social mobility and economic reality do not match', *Journal of Economic Behavior & Organization* 91, 75–92.

Bommier, A., Chassagnon, A. and Le Grand, F. (2012) 'Comparative risk aversion: a formal approach with applications to saving behavior', *Journal of Economic Theory* 147, 1614–1641.

Bradford, W.D. and Dolan, P. (2010) 'Getting used to it: the adaptive global utility model', *Journal of Health Economics* 29, 811–820.

Branas-Garza, P., Espinosa, M.P. and Rey-Biel, P. (2011) 'Travelers' types', *Journal of Economic Behavior & Organization* 78, 25–36.

Brekke, K.A. and Johansson-Stenman, O. (2008) 'The behavioural economics of climate change', *Oxford Review of Economic Policy* 24, 280–297.

Brown, A.L., Chua, Z.E. and Camerer, C.F. (2009) 'Learning and visceral temptation in dynamic saving experiments', *Quarterly Journal of Economics* 124, 197–231.

Bucchianeri, G.W. and Minson, J.A. (2013) 'A homeowner's dilemma: anchoring in residential real estate transactions', *Journal of Economic Behavior & Organization* 89, 76–92.

Bucciol, A., Houser, D. and Piovesan, M. (2011) 'Temptation and productivity: a field experiment with children', *Journal of Economic Behavior & Organization* 78, 126–136.

Burnham, T.C. (2013) 'Towards a neo-Darwinian synthesis of neoclassical and behavioral economics', *Journal of Economic Behavior and Organization* 90S, S113–S127.

Cadena, B.C. and Keys, B.J. (2013) 'Can self-control explain avoiding free money? Evidence from interest-free student loans', *Review of Economics and Statistics* 95, 1117–1129.

Campbell, J.Y. (2014) 'Empirical asset pricing: Eugene Fama, Lars Peter Hansen, and Robert Shiller', *Scandinavian Journal of Economics* 116, 593–634.

Cesarini, D., Dawes, C.T., Johannesson, M., Lichtenstein, P. and Wallace, B. (2009) 'Genetic variation in preferences for giving and risk taking', *Quarterly Journal of Economics* 142, 809–842.

Chandler, D. and Kapelner, A. (2013) 'Breaking monotony with meaning: motivation in crowdsourcing markets', *Journal of Economic Behavior & Organization* 90, 123–133.

Charness, G. and Dufwenberg, M. (2006) 'Promises and partnership', *Econometrica* 74, 1579–1601.

Charness, G., Gneezy, U. and Kuhn, M.A. (2013a) 'Experimental methods: extra-laboratory experiments – extending the reach of experimental economics', *Journal of Behavior & Organization* 91, 93–100.

Charness, G., Gneezy, U. and Imas, A. (2013b) 'Experimental methods: eliciting risk preferences', *Journal of Economic Behavior & Organization* 87, 43–51.

Cornelissen, T., Himmler, O. and Koenig, T. (2013) 'Fairness spillovers – the case of taxation', *Journal of Economic Behavior & Organization* 90, 164–180.

Corrigan, J.R., Rousu, M.C. and Depositario, D.P.T. (2014) 'Do practice rounds affect experimental auction results?' *Economic Letters* 123, 42–44.

Crawford, V.P. (2013) 'Boundedly rational versus optimization-based models of strategic thinking and learning in games', *Journal of Economic Literature* 51, 512–527.

Crettez, B. and Deloche, R. (2013) 'On experimental economics and the comparison between the last two versions of Moliere's Tartuffe', *Journal of Economic Behavior & Organization* 87, 66–72.

D'Exelle, B. and van den Berg, M. (2014) 'Aid distribution and cooperation in unequal communities', *Review of Income & Wealth* 60, 114–132.

D'Orlando, F. and Ferrante, F. (2009) 'The demand for job protection: some clues from behavioural economics', *Journal of Socio-Economics* 38, 104–114.

Datta, S. and Mullainathan, S. (2014) 'Behavioral design: a new approach to development policy', *Review of Income & Wealth* 60, 7–36.

De Clippel, G. (2014) 'Behavioral implementation', *American Economic Review* 104, 2975–3002.

De Coninck, J. (2011) 'Reinvigorating comparative law through behavioral economics? A cautiously optimistic view', *Review of Law & Economics* 7, 711–736.

Dellavigna, S. (2009) 'Psychology and economics: evidence from the field', *Journal of Economic Literature* 47, 315–372.

Dickhaut, J., Houser, D., Aimone, J.A., Tila, D. and Johnson, C. (2013a) 'High stakes behavior with low payoffs: inducing preferences with Holt-Laury gambles', *Journal of Economic Behavior & Organization* 94, 183–189.

Dickhaut, J., Smith, V., Xin, B. and Rustichini, A. (2013b) 'Human economic choice as costly information processing', *Journal of Economic Behavior & Organization* 94, 206–221.

Di Clemente, D.F. and Hantula, D.A. (2003) 'Applied behavioral economics and consumer choice', *Journal of Economic Psychology* 24, 589–602.

Di Guida, S., Marchiori, D. and Erev, I. (2012) 'Decisions among defaults and the effect of the option to do nothing', *Economics Letters* 117, 790–793.

Dohmen, T. (2014) 'Behavioral labor economics: advances and future directions', *Labour Economics* 30, 71–85.

Dufwenberg, M. and Gneezy, U. (2000) 'Measuring beliefs in an experimental lost wallet game', *Games & Economic Behavior* 30, 163–182.

Earl, P.E. (2011) 'From anecdotes to novels: reflective inputs for behavioural economics', *New Zealand Economic Papers* 45, 5–22.

Ellingsen, T. and Johannesson, M. (2004) 'Promises, threats and fairness', *Economic Journal* 114, 397–420.

Evren, O. (2012) 'Altruism and voting: a large-turnout result that does not rely on civic duty or cooperative behavior', *Journal of Economic Theory* 147, 2124–2157.

Fehr-Duda, H., Epper, T., Bruhin, A. and Schubert, R. (2011) 'Risk and rationality: the effects of mood and decision rules on probability weighting', *Journal of Economic Behavior & Organization* 78, 14–24.

Fenichel, E.P., Lupi, F., Hoehn, J.P. and Kaplowitz, M.D. (2009) 'Split-sample tests of "no opinion" responses in an attribute-based choice model', *Land Economics* 85, 348–362.

Finke, M.S. and Huston, S.J. (2013) 'Time preference and the importance of saving for retirement', *Journal of Economic Behavior & Organization* 89, 23–34.

Frantz, R. (2004) 'The behavioral economics of George Akerlof and Harvey Leibenstein', *Journal of Socio-Economics* 33, 29–44.

Frederick, S. (2005) 'Cognitive reflection and decision making', *Journal of Economic Perspectives* 19, 25–42.

Fudenberg, D. and Levine, D.K. (2012) 'Timing and self-control', *Econometrica* 80, 1–42.

Galai, D. and Sade, O. (2006) 'The ostrich effect and the relationship between the liquidity and the yields of financial assets', *Journal of Business* 79, 2741–2759.

Gherzi, S., Egan, D., Stewart, N., Haisley, E. and Ayton, P. (2014) 'The meerkat effect: personality and market returns affect investors' portfolio monitoring behaviour', *Journal of Economic Behavior & Organization* 107, 512–526.

Gowdy, J.M. (2008) 'Behavioral economics and climate change policy', *Journal of Economic Behavior & Organization* 68, 632–644.

Gul, F. and Pesendorfer, W. (2007) 'Welfare without happiness', *American Economic Review* 97, 471–476.

Gundersen, C., Schanzenbach, D.W. and Just, D.R. (2012) 'Insights into obesity from a behavioral economics perspective: discussion', *American Journal of Agricultural Economics* 94, 344–346.

Gunther, I. and Maier, J. (2014) 'Poverty, vulnerability, and reference-dependent utility', *Review of Income & Wealth* 60, 155–181.

Hadjiyiannis, C., Iris, D. and Tabakis, C. (2012) 'Multilateral tariff cooperation under fairness and reciprocity', *Canadian Journal of Economics* 45, 925–941.

Harrison, G.W., Martinez-Correa, J., Swarthout, J.T. (2013) 'Inducing risk neutral preferences with binary lotteries: a reconsideration', *Journal of Economic Behavior & Organization* 94, 145–159.

Harstad, R.M. and Selten. R. (2013) 'Bounded-rationality models: tasks to become intellectually competitive', *Journal of Economic Literature* 51, 496–511.

Harvey, C. Kelly, A., Morris, H. and Rowlinson, M. (2010) 'Academic Journal Quality Guide: Version 4', *The Association of Business Schools*, www.associationofbusinessschools.org/sites/default/files/Combined%20Journal%20Guide.pdf.

Hoffman, M., Lauer, T. and Rockenbach, B. (2013) 'The royal lie', *Journal of Economic Behavior & Organization* 93, 305–313.

Hyll, W. and Schneider, L. (2013) 'The causal effect of watching TV on material aspirations: evidence from the "valley of the innocent"', *Journal of Economic Behavior & Organization* 86, 37–51.

Ivanov, A., Levin, D. and Peck, J. (2013) 'Behavioral biases in endogenous-timing herding games: an experimental study', *Journal of Economic Behavior & Organization* 87, 25–34.

Jantti, M., Kanbur, R. and Pirttila, J. (2014a) 'Poverty, development and behavioral economics', *Review of Income & Wealth* 60, 1–6.

Jantti, M., Kanbur, R., Nyyssola, M. and Pirttila, J. (2014b) 'Poverty and welfare measurement on the basis of prospect theory', *Review of Income & Wealth* 60, 182–205.

Kahneman, D. and Tversky, A. (1979) 'Prospect theory: an analysis of decision under risk', *Econometrica* 47, 263–291.

Kallbekken, S., Kroll, S. and Cherry, T.L. (2011) 'Do you not like Pigou, or do you not understand him? Tax aversion and revenue recycling in the lab', *Journal of Environmental Economics & Management* 62, 53–64.

Kanbur, R., Pirttila, J. and Tuomala, M. (2008) 'Moral hazard, income taxation and prospect theory', *Scandinavian Journal of Economics* 110, 321–337.

Kandori, M. (1992) 'Social norms and community enforcement', *Review of Economic Studies* 59, 63–80.

Karlsson, N., Loewenstein, G. and Seppi, D. (2009) 'The ostrich effect: selective attention to information', *Journal of Risk & Uncertainty* 38, 95–115.

Kits, G.J., Adamowicz, W.L. and Boxall, P.C. (2014) 'Do conservation auctions crowd out voluntary environmentally friendly activities?', *Ecological Economics* 105, 118–123.

Kliger, D. van dem Assem, M.J. and Zwinkels, R.C.J. (2014) 'Empirical behavioral finance', *Journal of Economic Behavior & Organization* 107, 421–428.

Lindner, F. and Sutter, M. (2013) 'Level-k reasoning and time pressure in the 11–20 money request game', *Economics Letters* 120, 542–545.

Lightle, J.P. (2013) 'Harmful lie aversion and lie discovery in noisy expert advice games', *Journal of Economic Behavior & Organization* 93, 347–362.

List, J.A. and Samek, A.S. (2015) 'The behavioralist as nutritionist: leveraging behavioral economics to improve child food choice and consumption', *Journal of Health Economics* 39, 135–146.

Loewenstein, G., Read, D. and Bausmeister, R. (2003) *Time and Decision: Economic and Psychological Perspectives on Intertemporal Choice*, New York: Russell Sage Foundation.

Mandler, M. (2004) 'Status quo maintenance reconsidered: changing or incomplete preferences?', *Economic Journal* 114, 518–535.

Mandler, M. (2005) 'Incomplete preferences and rational transitivity of choice', *Games & Economic Behavior* 50, 255–277.

Mandler, M. (2014) 'Indecisiveness in behavioral welfare economics', *Journal of Economic Behavior & Organization* 97, 219–235.

Maskin, E. (1999) 'Nash equilibrium and welfare optimality', *Review of Economic Studies* 66, 23–38.

McAlvanah, P. (2010) 'Subadditivity, patience, and utility: the effects of dividing time intervals', *Journal of Economic Behavior & Organization* 76, 325–337.

McAlvanah, P. and Moul, C.C. (2013) 'The house doesn't always win: evidence of anchoring among Australian bookies', *Journal of Economic Behavior & Organization* 90, 87–99.

McCluskey, J.J., Mittelhammer, R.C. and Asiseh, F. (2011) 'From default to choice: adding healthy options to kids' menus', *American Journal of Agricultural Economics* 94, 338–343.

Miravete, E.J. and Palacios-Huerta, I. (2014) 'Consumer inertia, choice dependence, and learning from experience in a repeated decision problem', *Review of Economics & Statistics* 96, 524–537.

Oechssler, J., Roider, A. and Schmitz, P.W. (2009) 'Cognitive abilities and behavioral biases', *Journal of Economic Behavior & Organization* 72, 147–152.

Oreopoulos, P. and Salvanes, K.G. (2011) 'Priceless: the nonpecuniary benefits of schooling', *Journal of Economic Perspectives* 25, 159–184.

Pirinsky, C. (2013) 'Confidence and economic attitudes', *Journal of Economic Behavior & Organization* 91, 139–158.

Rabin, M. (2013a) 'Behavioral optimization models versus bounded-rationality models in decisions', *Journal of Economic Literature* 51, 528–43

Rabin, M. (2013b) 'An approach to incorporating psychology into economics', *American Economic Review* 103, 617–622.

Riener, G. and Wiederhold, S. (2013) 'Heterogeneous treatment effects in groups', *Economics Letters* 120, 408–412.

Rubinstein, A. (2007) 'Instinctive and cognitive reasoning: a study of response times', *Economic Journal* 117, 1243–1259.

Salant, Y. and Rubinstein, A. (2008) '(A, f) choice with frames', *Review of Economic Studies* 75, 1287–1296.

Sheremeta, R.M. and Shields, T.W. (2013) 'Do liars believe? Beliefs and other-regarding preferences in sender-receiver games', *Journal of Economic Behavior & Organization* 94, 268–277.

Shiller, R. (2014) 'Speculative asset prices', *American Economic Review*, 104, 1486–1517.

Sicherman, N., Loewenstein, G., Seppi, D. and Utkus, S. (2013) 'Financial attention', Working Paper.

Sloan, F.A., Eldred, L.M. and Xu, Y. (2014) 'The behavioral economics of drunk driving', *Journal of Health Economics* 35, 64–81.

Sorger, G. and Stark, O. (2013) 'Income redistribution going awry: the reversal power of the concern for relative deprivation', *Journal of Economic Behavior & Organization* 86, 1–9.

Spiegler, R. (2011) *Bounded Rationality and Industrial Organization*, New York: Oxford University Press.

Stahl, D.O. (2013) 'An experimental test of the efficacy of a simple reputation mechanism to solve social dilemmas', *Journal of Economic Behavior & Organization* 94, 116–212.

Stringham, E.P. (2011) 'Embracing morals in economics: the role of internal moral constraints in a market economy', *Journal of Economic Behavior & Organization* 78, 98–109.

Takanori, I. and Goto, R. (2009) 'Simultaneous measurement of time and risk preferences: stated preference discrete choice modeling analysis depending on smoking behavior', *International Economic Review* 50, 1169–1182.

Tonin, M. and Vlassopoulos, M. (2013) 'Experimental evidence of self-image concerns as motivation for giving', *Journal of Economic Behavior & Organization* 90, 19–27.

Tversky, A. and Kahneman, D. (1974) 'Judgment under uncertainty: heuristics and biases', *Science* 185, 1124–1130.

Van Hoorn, A. and Maseland, R. (2013) 'Does a Protestant work ethic exist? Evidence from the well-being effect of unemployment', *Journal of Economic Behavior & Organization* 91, 1–12.

Vanberg, C. (2008) 'Why do people keep their promises? An experimental test of two explanations', *Econometrica* 76, 1467–1480.

Volk, S., Thoni, C. and Ruigrok, W. (2012) 'Temporal stability and psychological foundations of cooperation preferences', *Journal of Economic Behavior & Organziation* 81, 664–676.

Weber, T.A. (2012) 'An augmented Becker-DeGroot-Marshak mechanism for transaction cycles', *Economics Letters* 114, 43–46.

Wrede, M. (2011) 'Hyperbolic discounting and fertility', *Journal of Population Economics* 24, 1053–1070.

Zubrickas, R. (2012) 'How exposure to markets can favor inequity-averse preferences', *Journal of Economic Behavior & Organization* 84, 174–181.

3 Recent developments in the bounded rationality literature

A survey

As with the review of the behavioural economics literature in the previous chapter, the survey of the bounded rationality literature presented here focuses on the recent developments in the literature rather than on the literature as a whole. With this in mind, the survey that follows focuses in particular on the relevant articles identified in the same online literature search using the *EBSCOhost Online Research Database*, examining each journal in the *Association of Business Schools Academic Journal Quality Guide* (version 4: see Harvey *et al.*, 2010) using 'bounded rationality' as the designated subject term. These articles, which were generally published between 2007 and 2015, are outlined in Appendix 3.1.

The taxonomy used to structure the review is displayed in Figure 3.1. It is immediately evident that this literature is much less diverse than that relating to behavioural economics (comparing Figure 3.1 with Figure 2.1 in the previous chapter). Indeed, works within the bounded rationality literature can be effectively separated into two categories: investigation and survey. Each of these is examined below.

Investigation

'Investigation' articles within the bounded rationality literature are identified as those that examine the consequences of the discrepancy between the complexity of the decisions that decision-makers are required to make, on the one hand, and the cognitive abilities of those decision-makers, on the other. Following the suggested taxonomy in Mallard (2012), these can be further subdivided into five categories according to the nature of the decision being made, which are also identified in Figure 3.1.

Standard choice

The traditional view of the decision-making process is that it consists of three stages. Decision-makers firstly acquire relevant information (step 1), which they then process (step 2) in order to identify their response or choice (step 3). Mallard (2012) presents a taxonomy of the approaches to modelling bounded rationality that are based on this three-step process, demonstrating that works of bounded rationality have restricted a decision-maker's ability to make decisions optimally by imposing

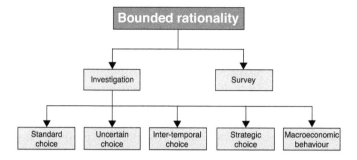

Figure 3.1 Bounded rationality: a general taxonomy

constraints at each of these three steps. This provides a helpful structure for the discussion of works of bounded rationality that relate to situations of standard choice: situations in which a decision-maker is required to make a choice from a range of certain, current options that generate immediate payoffs. However, it should be stressed that categorising works according to these three types of constraints is not precise (and is indeed a little arbitrary in the case of certain works); and that, in addition to these three categories, there are also works that specifically examine how an individual's preferences can be elicited from observations of behaviour in such decision situations; these are discussed at the end.

The first type of decision-making constraint, then, is that imposed on the relevant information that is available to the individual. For example, Mackowiak and Wiederholt (2012) examine the behaviour of decision-makers who are required to acquire and process costly information to make their decisions. These authors find that decision-makers who are characterised by limited liability (thereby bounding the potential losses to which they are exposed) choose to acquire and process less information than those with unlimited liability, and that this result is strengthened as the cost of information acquisition rises. Adopting a similar approach, Matejka and McKay (2012) present a model of consumer search in which the consumer is 'rationally inattentive', which in this situation means that the consumer knows all the available sellers in the market but is not fully aware of the terms that they each offer. The consumer can decide to evaluate any of the offers, and can do so with any degree of precision and by employing any search process; but the consumer faces a cost of acquiring more precise information about what the sellers are offering. The authors find that, among other things, as the cost of information acquisition falls, the market price falls to the competitive level; when the cost of information acquisition is different across the consumers, low-quality firms set high prices; and when the cost of information acquisition is the same for the consumers, prices increase with quality. As a final example of this approach, Chen and Zhang (2011) examine a model in which each consumer demands at most one unit of a product; some of the consumers are informed about the relevant market prices and so purchase from the seller offering the lowest price, while others are uninformed and search for the price information they require: some performing multiple searches sequentially in an optimal fashion (the optimal searchers) while the others search only once (the boundedly rational searchers). The authors find that equilibrium prices may be characterised by clusters of high and low prices; may be reduced if the reservation price of the boundedly rational searchers falls beneath that of the optimal searchers; and may be increased due to a reduction in the cost of searching for price information.

Salant (2011) adopts the second approach, of constraining the ability of the decision-maker to process the available information, by employing an automaton to implement a number of different choice rules, measuring the complexity of each choice rule by the number of states that the automaton requires to implement it. The author finds that any choice rule that is simpler than the standard assumption of utility maximisation is subject to framing effects and that any choice rule that results from an optimal trade-off between utility maximisation and complexity are history-dependent satisficing procedures that are sensitive to the order in which the options are presented. In a related paper, Manzini and Mariotti (2007) present a model in which a decision-maker sequentially employs two choice rules in order to select from the available options: rules that are implemented in a fixed order, independent of the choice set, to remove inferior alternatives (the first rule identifies a short list of options from which the second rule then chooses). The authors define a 'rational shortlist method' as a choice function that identifies a final option that can be identified by such a two-step, sequential decision-making process; and demonstrate that it is possible to test whether or not observed choices are compatible with a rational shortlist method, and that a rational shortlist method procedure is able to explain a number of the behavioural anomalies that have been identified in the literature. Other works that model decision-makers as being characterised by process constraints include Tutino (2013), Tyson (2008) and Jerger and Michaelis (2011). Tutino (2013) examines risk-averse consumers who rationally choose both the quantity and the quality of information to process about their wealth in the face of processing constraints; finding that consumption responses to wealth shocks are asymmetric, with negative shocks producing faster and stronger reaction than positive shocks, and that information-processing constraints increase persistence and volatility of consumption behaviour. Tyson (2008) examines the behaviour of a decision-maker whose cognitive limitations, at least in part, prevent him from perceiving his own preferences among the available options: an effect that is assumed to be increasing with the complexity of the choice problem. Assuming that complexity is aligned with set inclusion leads to the violation of the contraction consistency axiom of the standard model of rational choice. As a final example, Jerger and Michaelis (2011) explain the 'fixed wage puzzle' (the observation that profit-sharing arrangements are rarely used despite being Pareto-superior to fixed wage contracts) in a model in which employers and employees use simplifying heuristics when processing the contracting options.

Eliaz and Rubinstein (2014) present a model in which a decision-maker is constrained in terms of the responses that he can make. More specifically, it is a model in which each individual in a population chooses one of two options, but in which the individuals do not know what the available options are and so can choose an option only after observing another individual doing so. This means that individuals can choose to either imitate another individual or to wait until he has observed two individuals choosing differently, enabling him to compare the options and to choose accordingly. In the first case that is examined, the decision-maker notices whether the individual he observes has imitated others or whether he actually compared the available options. In the second, the decision-maker instead notices whether or not the observed individual's decision was hasty. The authors find that in equilibrium the probability that the decision-maker chooses mistakenly is higher in the second case and that the existence of these nonstandard 'neuro' observations (the additional information regarding the choice processes of the observed individuals) systematically biases the equilibrium outcome.

Finally, there are those models of standard choice situations that examine how preferences can be elicited from observed choice behaviour. For example, Papi (2013) examines decision-making that is based on a search process and that employs a satisficing stopping condition in order to assess the understanding that can be garnered about both the levels of satisfaction and the preferences of decision-makers from observing varying amounts of information about such a choice procedure. Manzini and Mariotti (2014) examine a different choice procedure, one based on the two-step decision process of Eliaz and Spiegler (2011), in which a decision-maker considers each feasible option with a given (unobservable) probability (what they refer to as the 'attention parameter') and then chooses the considered option that maximises his preference function. The authors demonstrate how an observer of choice frequencies can test whether or not the choices they observe are generated by such a rule of behaviour and, if it is, how preferences can be inferred. Masatlioglu *et al.* (2012) examine when and how an individual's preferences (and also the options that he does and does not consider) can be elicited from choices observed in a similar setting, when the individual does not consider all the available options; finding that welfare judgements can be misleading when the underlying choice procedure is not specified. Finally, Rubinstein and Salant (2012) examine how preferences can be elicited from observed choices that may differ between situations even though the situations are not different in any way that is relevant to the payoffs of the available choices.

Uncertain choice

Decision situations of uncertain choice are those in which an individual is required to choose between a set of available options while not being wholly sure about the payoffs from each. For example, Yao and Li (2013) study a model in which investors seek to maximise the value of the not-fully-known returns from their investments. The authors demonstrate that the behavioural traits of loss aversion and optimism can be beneficial in terms of increasing the returns on investment in such situations; and so, for individuals characterised by bounded rationality, loss aversion and optimism may naturally arise in situations of decision-making under uncertainty. Stranlund and Ben-Haim (2008) present an analysis in which environmental policy options in situations of uncertainty are intended to achieve a satisficing level of welfare loss from the uncertainty rather than seeking to achieve expected welfare maximisation.

Inter-temporal choice

Inter-temporal decision-making involves an individual making a choice in the present that does not bring a payoff until some time in the future, in a situation that may be one of strategic choice. For example, Miao (2010) presents a dynamic model of the strategic interaction between consumers on the one hand and either a monopoly or a pair of duopolies on the other, in order to examine the behaviour of myopic consumers who optimise period-by-period, without giving any consideration to information about future periods. The author finds that producers are able to monopolise 'aftermarkets' (markets for the complementary goods that are required for the good purchased in the primary market, such as the market for ink in relation to that for photocopiers) by strategically making their primary goods compatible with only the complementary goods they sell; and that a pair of duopolies earn positive profits from across both markets despite engaging in price competition with undifferentiated products in the primary market. Arango and Moxnes (2012) study experimentally the effects of bounded rationality that arises from the complexity of an investment decision (in terms of the lifetime of the investment and also the length of the time lag between investment and production) on the cyclical nature of a cobweb model; finding that the cyclicality of the market price worsens as the complexity of the decision is increased. The final two examples of such papers are those by Binswanger (2010, 2012), which examine aspects of savings behaviour. Binswanger (2010) employs a bounded rationality model (the 'feasibility-goals model') to explain why savings behaviour varies with income levels to the extent that it does. The element of bounded rationality in this model is that the savers are assumed to seek to make certain levels of consumption feasible in possible future states, rather than requiring them to engage in contingent planning (which requires them to anticipate their actions in each possible state of the future). Binswanger (2012) presents a related model (the 'hierarchical feasibility goals model'), which assumes that savers, characterised by procedural rationality, seek to achieve a list of hierarchically ordered goals. The author asserts that this model better explains how the proportion of savings invested in stocks varies over the lifecycle and that its predictions are consistent with other patterns in the data; for example, its prediction that both savings and equity shares increase with current and permanent income, and that the young either hold no equity or their equity holding is low and then increases over their working life.

Strategic choice

Strategic choice refers to decision-making in situations in which the choice of one decision-maker is predicated on the choices that he expects to be made by others: to game theoretic situations in which decision-makers engage in inter-related decision-making. The two most prominent ways in which bounded rationality is integrated into such analyses are the *cognitive hierarchy* (or *level-k*) and the *quantal response equilibrium* approaches (Rogers *et al.*, 2009). These are discussed in turn, before moving onto other related works in the literature.

The cognitive hierarchy approach was first presented in Stahl and Wilson (1995). In these models, and those of level-*k* reasoning, each player engages in a specific number of discrete steps of reasoning, according to which he is categorised. The assumption that players respond optimally is maintained, but moderated by assuming that different players are able to process the relevant information to different degrees. Players characterised by level-0 reasoning lie at the bottom of the hierarchy and behave in a completely random fashion; the level-1 types are able to eliminate dominated strategies but do not believe other players will do the same; the level-2 types eliminate dominated strategies and believe that other players will do likewise, and so on up the hierarchy. The difference between cognitive hierarchy models and those of level-*k* reasoning is that players in the former possess accurate beliefs about the relative frequencies of those below them in the hierarchy, whereas those in the latter are able to look only one step down. Works that have adopted this approach include those of Crawford and Iriberri (2007) and Arad and Rubinstein (2012). The first of these demonstrates that a model of level-*k* reasoning can effectively explain both the winner's curse in common-value auctions and over-bidding in independent-private-value auctions, concluding that the level-*k* approach allows a large body of data from auction experiments to be linked to findings from other experiments designed to study strategic thinking. The second presents a new experimental test of level-*k* reasoning: the 11–20 money request game (mentioned above), in which each player has to request an amount between 11 and 20 shekels, which he will receive with certainty plus an additional 20 shekels if he requests exactly one shekel less than the other player. The authors find from testing this procedure on students that players tend to exhibit at most three levels of reasoning; and two further variants of the game demonstrate that the depth of reasoning is not increased by enhancing the attractiveness of the level-0 strategy or by reducing the cost of undercutting the other player.

The quantal response equilibrium (QRE) approach to integrating bounded rationality into strategic decision-making, which originated in the work of Luce (1959), has been interpreted in contrasting ways in the literature. For example, McKelvey and Palfrey (1995) and Rogers *et al.* (2009) assert that it maintains the assumption that players respond optimally but that their payoffs include unobserved disturbance; whereas Chen *et al.* (1997) argue that it assumes players cannot properly evaluate the utility payoffs from each of the available options and so they 'better-respond' instead, choosing strategies with higher expected payoffs with greater probability. Rogers *et al.* (2009) present two different QRE models, in each of which the skill levels of the players (their payoff responsiveness) and their beliefs about the skill levels of the other players varies across the players. In one version, the players share common and correct information about the distribution of skill levels across players, whereas in the second, this distribution is not common knowledge and beliefs about skill levels are instead downward looking (meaning that players believe that their skill levels are superior to those of others). The authors demonstrate that doing this connects the cognitive hierarchy approach above with the QRE approach: more specifically, that the cognitive hierarchy model is a limiting case of the second type of model. Testing these different models empirically, the authors find significant evidence that both skill and cognitive levels differ across players, and also of downward-looking beliefs (at least in some of the games). In a related study, Le Coq and Sturluson (2013) adopt the QRE approach and demonstrate that the findings from laboratory experiments that individuals consistently choose investment levels above the subgame-perfect equilibrium level in pre-commitment games can be attributed to players' perceptions of the rationality (skill) levels of the other players. The authors support this assertion with observations from an experiment in which a player's level of experience is used as a proxy for his level of rationality; demonstrating that an individual's behaviour differs significantly depending on the experience of the other players: that facing inexperienced players tends to induce individuals to choose higher investments. A final example of this approach is that of Golman (2011), which demonstrates that the aggregate behaviour of a population of players employing different quantal response functions can be modelled with a representative agent.

There also exist numerous alternative approaches to investigating the effects of bounded rationality in strategic decision-making within the literature. Again following the taxonomy presented in Mallard (2012), these can be categorised according to the nature of the constraints imposed on the players' decision-making, namely: information constraints, processing constraints and response constraints.

Eyster and Rabin (2005) impose information constraints on the players within their model. More specifically, players possess correct information about the marginal distribution of each other player's type and about the marginal distribution of each other player's action, but they do not possess correct information about the correlation between the two. In the extreme, 'fully cursed', equilibrium, players believe there to be no correlation; while in a 'partially cursed' equilibrium, players believe there to be some correlation. The authors identify a range of partially cursed equilibria that explains the experiments they analyse more effectively than the standard model of rational choice. In a similar approach, the players in the model of Jehiel and Koessler (2007) possess correct information about the average behaviour of the other players over collections of states (what the authors call 'analogy classes') but not about the strategies that other players employ in each state. Players extract the simplest information that is consistent with their observations and they expect that other players also condition their strategies on analogy classes rather than on specific states, which leads to the 'analogy-based expectation equilibrium'. Miettinen (2009) demonstrates the link between the partially cursed equilibrium of Eyster and Rabin (2005) and the analogy-based expectation equilibrium of Jehiel and Koessler (2007). Other works that impose information constraints on decision-makers in situations of strategic choice include those of Krasa and Williams (2007) and Wilson (2014). In the first of these, the authors examine contracting when individuals possess only limited observability (being unable to observe all the relevant information) and they find that a contract between such individuals is necessarily finite (and so suboptimal), but that there are conditions in which an optimal contract can be achieved as the limit of a sequence of finite contracts; whereas in the second, the author demonstrates through a dynamic game that characterising decision-makers with limited recall (bounded memory) can rationalise certain behavioural anomalies, such as salience and confirmation bias.

Other works adopt the approach of constraining the ability of players to process the information that is relevant to the situation in which they find themselves. For example, Halpern and Pass (2015) adopt the approach of Rubinstein (1986) in examining the behaviour of players who choose a machine to play a game on their behalf (in this case a Turing machine rather than a finite automaton). The authors find that in this framework, in which there are two elements of complexity (the sophistication of the machine employed and the complexity of the information it receives), certain standard outcomes of game theory do not hold (for example, the existence of Nash equilibria and the revelation principle) and that certain behavioural anomalies (such as cooperation in a finitely repeated prisoners' dilemma game) arise naturally. Kalayci and Potters (2011) experimentally examine the effects of increasing consumer confusion (through sellers who are able to increase the number of the attributes of their goods that they announce to consumers, which has no effect on the value of the goods) on market prices, finding that consumers make more suboptimal choices and that the prices of the goods are higher, with a greater number of announced attributes. A final example of this approach in strategic choice analysis is that of Esponda (2008), which presents a new theoretical solution concept for analysing games in which players are naïve, in the sense that they fail to account for the informational content of the actions of the other players: the players may learn from experience but they do not realise how that learning would have been different if they had acted differently.

Finally, there are those works that impose response constraints on decision-makers within strategic choice situations. For example, consider the works of Eliaz and Spiegler (2011) and Glazer and Rubinstein (2012). In the first of these, the authors examine a game played between consumers and firms, in which consumers possess standard preferences but not complete knowledge about the set of available options, instead having 'consideration sets' (sets of available options that they perceive to be relevant to them) from which they make their choices; and in which the firms are able to manipulate the consideration sets of consumers. Assuming that the firms have the objective of maximising their market share minus their fixed costs, the authors find that as long as costs are not too high, there exist equilibria in which firms earn the same profits that they would earn if consumers were rational; in the symmetric equilibria with rational-consumer profit levels, there is perfect correlation between a firm persuading a consumer to consider a new product and persuading him to buy it; and industry profits are not necessarily monotonically decreasing with the degree of consumer rationality. In the second, the authors constrain the options that a decision-maker is able to choose. More specifically, the authors examine a model in which a listener announces a set of conditions that need to be satisfied if he is to be persuaded by the information that the speaker presents. Following this commitment, the speaker then chooses which information to present: either his true profile or a dishonest profile. The authors introduce bounded rationality in the responses that are available to the speaker by making them determined by the speaker's true profile, the content of the announced conditions and the way in which the conditions are framed. The authors provide some experimental evidence in support of the argument that the model captures some elements of real life. The authors examine the nature of the optimal set of conditions to announce in such a situation, which leads to implications for mechanism design with boundedly rational agents.

Macroeconomic behaviour

A number of papers in the bounded rationality literature have widened the scope of analysis, examining the macroeconomic effects of boundedly rational behaviour. For example, Sordi and Vercelli (2012) examine the effects that simple (boundedly rational) rules for the formation of expectations (rather than the assumption of rational expectations) have on Minsky's *financial instability hypothesis*. The authors demonstrate that the widespread use of extrapolative expectations by economic agents within an economy produces a high degree of financial instability, which may lead to a financial crisis, and that the widespread use of a mix of extrapolative and regressive expectations reduces the instability of the model but may give rise to complex dynamics. In a related paper, Fehr and Tyran (2008) examine when rational agents are decisive in market outcomes and when those characterised by bounded rationality shape the outcome. Examining a situation in which nominal prices adjust after an anticipated monetary shock, the authors find that bounded rationality is important in the aggregate adjustment as it causes inertia in the adjustment of nominal prices. Of particular importance in this regard is money illusion (which the authors define as the use by economic agents of nominal incomes as a proxy for real incomes) and anchoring (which they define as agents adjusting their behaviour from salient reference points). However, the authors also find that the strategic environment is important: if the actions of agents are strategic substitutes, nominal price adjustment is quick; but if they are strategic complements, the adjustment is slow and is associated with significant real effects.

Fazzari *et al.* (2010) and Arifovic *et al.* (2010) both examine the effect of bounded rationality on the effectiveness of monetary policy. In the first of these papers, the authors examine monetary policy in a reduced-form dynamic stochastic general equilibrium (DSGE) model with bounded rationality (included as AR(1) expectations processes, calibrated so that they change with relevant model parameters) and an empirically motivated investment function. The authors find that the cost of capital effect on investment is more important for monetary transmission than the more widely studied inter-temporal consumption substitution parameter; and that a strong Taylor rule response to unemployment in this model is more effective in stabilising demand-induced fluctuations than a strong response to inflation; indeed, an excessively aggressive response to inflation increases the simulated output and inflation fluctuations. In the second paper, the authors examine the potential commitment value of cheap talk (non-binding information) announcements in a situation in which the economic agents either believe an announcement (thereby setting their inflation forecasts equal to the rate announced) or not believe (and so employ adaptive learning to forecast inflation, potentially all generating different forecasts), switching between these two strategies based on information they receive about the associated payoffs. The authors demonstrate that the policy-maker learns to sustain a situation with a positive fraction of believers, that this outcome is Pareto superior to the outcome predicted by standard theory and that the actions of the policy-maker alter in response to the heterogeneity among and learning of the agents.

Survey papers

As in the behavioural economics literature, a number of papers within the bounded rationality literature present surveys of the field. However, whereas those of behavioural economics can be further categorised as developmental, analytical and suggestive surveys (see Chapter 2), those of bounded rationality are generally of the analytical type. This means they critically examine either the literature as a whole according to particular criteria or more specific facets of the field and the lessons that have been learned from them: particularly the former. For example, Harstad and Selten (2013) present an evaluative survey of the bounded rationality literature as a whole, particularly focusing on the ways in which it is still not a viable replacement for the standard model of rational choice and the ways in which it needs to make further progress. The authors argue that the standard rational choice framework is still the dominant approach because of its range of applicability; its coherence, internal structure and teachability; its isolation of economic forces and definitiveness; its solution concepts and stationarity; its ability to streamline and focus empirical and econometric studies; and the efficiency of its conclusions and its minimal use of value judgements. All of these advantages can perhaps be summarised by saying that it remains the dominant approach because of its parsimony. However, the authors assert that it is too early to conclude that bounded rationality cannot attain these characteristics; and that a key part in realising this is greater integration of theory and empirics. A second example of this is Rabin (2013), in which the author outlines a case for integrating the findings of psychology about decision-making into economics through optimisation models. In particular, the author argues that bounded rationality does not just arise because of the computational complexity of optimisation (what the author calls 'bounds errors'), although it is undeniable that this is a cause: it also arises because decision-makers are attracted to the 'suboptimal' outcome (what the author calls 'astray errors'). These latter cases are readily modelled through optimisation: by adjusting the nature of the preference function or the beliefs that decision-makers form about the available options. A third example is Mehta (2013), which is a critical survey of the discourse surrounding bounded rationality within the wider economics literature. The author draws on the literature to argue that the discourse pathologises consumers who are susceptible to suboptimal market outcomes, treating their behaviour as abnormal and treating them as deviants in need of rehabilitation. Furthermore, this discourse leads to new forms of policy being legitimised; more specifically, behavioural remedies designed to draw apparently errant consumers towards behaviour that conforms more closely to the standard model of rational choice. The author argues that the upsurge of interest in these behavioural remedies distracts attention from facets of the individual's environment, such as the characteristics of markets and the behaviour of firms, and also the set of norms and beliefs underpinning the economic system.

References

Arad, A. and Rubinstein, A. (2012) 'The 11–20 money request game: a level-k reasoning study', *American Economic Review* 102, 3561–3573.

Arango, S. and Moxnes, E. (2012) 'Commodity cycles, a function of market complexity? Extending the cobweb experiment', *Journal of Economic Behavior & Organization* 84, 321–334.

Arifovic, J., Dawid, H., Deissenberg, C. and Kostyshyna, O. (2010) 'Learning benevolent leadership in a heterogenous agents economy', *Journal of Economic Dynamics and Control* 34, 1768–1790.

Binswanger, J. (2010) 'Understanding the heterogeneity of savings and asset allocation: a behavioral-economics perspective', *Journal of Economic Behavior & Organization* 76, 296–317.

Binswanger, J. (2012) 'Life cycle saving: insights from the perspective of bounded rationality', *European Economic Review* 56, 605–623.

Chen, H.-C., J.W. Friedman and Thisse, J.-F. (1997) 'Boundedly rational Nash Equilibrium: a probabilistic choice approach', *Games & Economic Behavior* 18, 32–54.

Chen, Y. and Zhang, T. (2011) 'Equilibrium price dispersion with heterogeneous searchers', *International Journal of Industrial Organization* 29, 645–654.

Crawford, V.P. and Iriberri, N. (2007) 'Level-k auctions: can a nonequilibrium model of strategic thinking explain the winner's curse and overbidding in private-value auctions?', *Econometrica* 75, 1721–1770.

Eliaz, K. and Rubinstein, A. (2014) 'A model of boundedly rational "neuro" agents', *Economic Theory* 57, 515–528.

Eliaz, K. and Spiegler, R. (2011) 'Consideration sets and competitive marketing', *Review of Economic Studies* 78, 235–262.

Esponda, I. (2008) 'Behavioral equilibrium in economies with adverse selection', *American Economic Review* 98(4), 1269–1291.

Eyster, E. and Rabin, M. (2005) 'Cursed equilibrium', *Econometrica* 73, 1623–1672.

Fazzari, S.M., Ferri, P. and Greenberg, E. (2010) 'Investment and the Taylor Rule in a dynamic Keynesian model', *Journal of Economic Dynamics & Control* 34, 2010–2022.

Fehr, E. and Tyran, J.-R. (2008) 'Limited rationality and strategic interaction: the impact of the strategic environment on nominal inertia', *Econometrica* 76, 353–394.

Glazer, J. and Rubinstein, A. (2012) 'A model of persuasion with boundedly rational agents', *Journal of Political Economy* 120, 1057–1082.

Golman, R. (2011) 'Quantal response equilibria with heterogeneous agents', *Journal of Economic Theory* 146, 2013–2028.

Halpern, J.Y. and Pass, R. (2015) 'Algorithmic rationality: game theory with costly computation', *Journal of Economic Theory* 156, 246–268.

Harstad, R.M. and Selten, R. (2013) 'Bounded-rationality models: tasks to become intellectually competitive', *Journal of Economic Literature* 51, 496–511.

Harvey, C. Kelly, A., Morris, H. and Rowlinson, M. (2010) 'Academic Journal Quality Guide: Version 4', *The Association of Business Schools*, www.associationofbusinessschools.org/sites/default/files/Combined%20Journal%20Guide.pdf.

Jehiel, P. and Koessler, F. (2007) 'Revisiting games of incomplete information with analogy based expectations', *Games & Economic Behavior* 62, 533–557.

Jerger, J. and Michaelis, J. (2011) 'The fixed wage puzzle: why profit sharing is so hard to implement', *Economics Letters* 110, 104–106.

Kalayci, K. and Potters, J. (2011) 'Buyer confusion and market prices', *International Journal of Industrial Organization* 29, 14–22.

Krasa, S. and Williams, S.R. (2007) 'Limited observability as a constraint in contract design', *Journal of Economic Theory* 134, 379–404.

Le Coq, C. and Sturluson, J.T. (2013) 'Does opponents' experience matter? Experimental evidence from a quantity precommitment game', *Journal of Economic Behavior & Organization* 84, 265–277.

Luce, R.D. (1959) *Individual Choice Behavior: A Theoretical Analysis*, New York: John Wiley

Mackowiak, B. and Wiederholt, M. (2012) 'Information processing and limited liability', *American Economic Review Papers and Proceedings* 102, 30–34.

Mallard, G. (2012) 'Modelling cognitively bounded rationality: an evaluative taxonomy', *Journal of Economic Surveys* 26, 674–704.

Manzini, P. and Mariotti, M. (2007) 'Sequentially rationalizable choice', *American Economic Review* 97, 1824–1839.

Manzini, P. and Mariotti, M. (2014) 'Stochastic choice and consideration sets', *Econometrica* 82, 1153–1176.

Masatlioglu, Y., Nakajima, D. and Ozbay, E.Y. (2012) 'Revealed attention', *American Economic Review* 102, 2183–2205.

Matejka, F. and McKay, A. (2012) 'Simple market equilibria with rationally inattentive consumers', *American Economic Review Papers and Proceedings* 102, 24–29.

McKelvey, R.D. and Palfrey, T.R. (1995) 'Quantal response equilibria for normal form games', *Games & Economic Behavior* 10, 6–38.

Mehta, J. (2013) 'The discourse of bounded rationality in academic and policy arenas: pathologising the errant consumer', *Cambridge Journal of Economics* 37, 1243–1261.

Miao, C.-H. (2010) 'Consumer myopia, standardization and aftermarket monopolization', *European Economic Review* 54, 931–946.

Miettinen, T. (2009) 'The partially cursed and the analogy-based expectation equilibrium', *Economics Letters* 105, 162–164.

Papi, M. (2013) 'Satisficing choice procedures', *Journal of Economic Behavior & Organization* 84, 451–462.

Rogers, B.W., Palfrey, T.R. and Camerer, C.F. (2009) 'Heterogeneous quantal response equilibrium and cognitive hierarchies', *Journal of Economic Theory* 144, 1440–1467.

Rabin, M. (2013) 'Incorporating limited rationality into economics', *Journal of Economic Literature* 51, 528–543.

Rubinstein, A. (1986) 'Finite automata play the repeated prisoner's dilemma', *Journal of Economic Theory* 39, 83–96.

Rubinstein, A. and Salant, Y. (2012) 'Eliciting welfare preferences from behavioural data sets', *Review of Economic Studies* 79, 375–387.

Salant, Y. (2011) 'Procedural analysis of choice rules with applications to bounded rationality', *American Economic Review* 101, 724–748.

Sordi, S. and Vercelli, A. (2012) 'Heterogeneous expectations and strong uncertainty in a Minskyian model of financial fluctuations', *Journal of Economic Behavior & Organization* 83, 544–557.

Stahl, D.O. and Wilson, P. (1995) 'On players' models of other players: theory and experimental evidence', *Games & Economic Behavior* 10, 218–54.

Stranlund, J.K. and Y. Ben-Haim (2008) 'Price-based vs. quantity-based environmental regulation under Knightian uncertainty: an info-gap robust satisficing perspective', *Journal of Environmental Management* 87, 443–49.

Tutino, A. (2013) 'Rationally inattentive consumption choice', *Review of Economic Dynamics* 16, 421–439.

Tyson, C.J. (2008) 'Cognitive constraints, contraction consistency, and the satisficing criterion', *Journal of Economic Theory* 138, 51–71.

Wilson, A. (2014) 'Bounded memory and biases in information processing', *Econometrica* 82, 2257–2294.

Yao, J. and Li, D. (2013) 'Bounded rationality as a source of loss aversion and optimism: a study of psychological adaptation under incomplete information', *Journal of Economic Dynamics & Control* 37, 18–31.

4 Audiences and impacts

The purpose of this chapter is to examine the behavioural economics and bounded rationality literatures in terms of their intended audiences and the academic standing of their works within the wider economics discipline. To do this, the following three questions are considered:

1 What is the nature of the economics academic journals in which articles on behavioural economics and bounded rationality tend to be published?
2 What is the academic standing of the economics academic journals in which articles on behavioural economics and bounded rationality tend to be published?
3 What is the impact, in terms of the number of citations, of articles on behavioural economics and bounded rationality within the wider literature?

As with the surveys presented in the previous chapters, the literatures are too large to take every relevant publication into account, especially the vast literature on behavioural economics. As such, the analysis that follows in this chapter is restricted to the relevant articles identified in the same online literature search as that in the previous chapters, using the *EBSCOhost Research Database* to examine each academic journal in the economics section of the *Association of Business Schools Academic Journal Quality Guide* (version 4, see Harvey *et al.*, 2010) in turn, using 'behavioural economics' and 'bounded rationality' as the designated subject terms. This process identified 347 relevant articles, which are outlined in the appendices to Chapters 2 and 3.

Publications by journal

The first observation to make about the online search of the literatures is that the behavioural economics literature is significantly larger than that of bounded rationality: with 254 and 93 relevant articles, respectively. Although these figures are specific to the particular search undertaken for the purposes of this monograph, this observation is representative of the wider literatures as a whole.

The second observation, which is apparent from Figures 4.1 and 4.2, is that the publication of behavioural economics articles is characterised by a rough bell curve

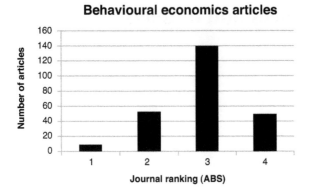

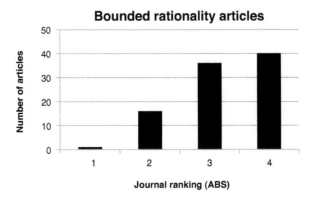

Figure 4.1 Behavioural economics and bounded rationality articles by *ABS* journal ranking (absolute figures)

distribution according to the ranking of the journal. The greatest concentration of behavioural economics articles (55 per cent) is found within the journals that hold a level 3 ranking within the *Association of Business Schools* (*ABS*) journal rankings, which are often defined as presenting research of 'international signif-icance'; with 20 per cent and 21 per cent of behavioural economics articles being published in level 4 and level 2 journals, respectively. This picture is different for the bounded rationality articles. The highest proportion of bounded rationality articles (43 per cent) is published within level 4 journals, which are often defined as presenting 'world leading research', with 39 per cent published in level 3 journals and 17 per cent in level 2 journals. The implication of this is that articles of bounded rationality, when they are accepted for publication, tend to have a higher academic standing within the economics literature as a whole than those of behavioural economics as a greater proportion are published within the highest level of journals. A possible explanation for this lies in the fact that the level 4 journals tend to be generalist journals, presenting world leading work that is applicable to economics widely, whereas the level 3 journals tend to be more field specific: for example, the *Journal of Health Economics*, the *Journal of Development Economics* and the *Journal of Population Economics* (this is not without exception, of course: the *Journal of Environmental Economics & Management* and the *Journal of Risk & Uncertainty* are both classified as level 4 journals within the ABS rankings). As such, the more theoretical approach of bounded rationality, examining decision-making in a general framework, perhaps has a closer fit to the level 4 journals given its less field-specific focus; whereas articles of behavioural economics, which tend to focus on specific types of decisions and specific situations, arguably have a closer fit with the level 3 journals. This result can also be explained, at least partially, by the observation that the *Journal of Economic Behavior & Organization*, in which by far the greatest proportion of behavioural economics articles in this sample are published (85, which accounts for 33 per cent of the entire sample), is a level 3 journal.

Examining this pattern of publication more finely, further observations can be made. Of the behavioural economics articles in the sample, 29 per cent of those published in level 4 journals appear in the two journals considered to be most theoretical in nature (*Econometrica* and the *Journal of Economic Theory*), whilst 22 per cent of these articles are published in the two level 4 journals that present the most survey and opinion-based articles (the *Journal of Economic Literature* and the *Journal of Economic Perspectives*). Of the bounded rationality articles in the sample, these proportions are 43 per cent and 10 per cent, respectively. This further buttresses the interpretation that the bounded rationality approach is more theoretical and less interpretative in nature than the field of behavioural economics.

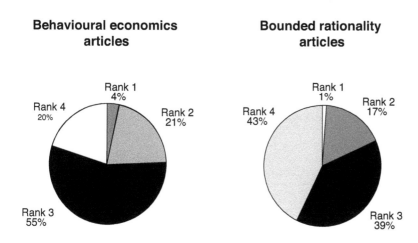

Figure 4.2 Behavioural economics and bounded rationality articles by *ABS* journal ranking (percentages)

Citations of articles

The number of citations that a published article receives can be taken to represent the impact of the article within the wider literature. In order to address the last of the three questions opening this chapter, then, the numbers of citations that the articles within the literature sample have received is subjected to ordinary least squares regression analysis. More specifically, equation (4.1) is estimated:

$$Citations = \alpha + \beta_1 \, Rank + \beta_2 \, Time + \beta_3 \, Category + \epsilon \qquad (4.1)$$

'Citations' refers to the number of citations that each article has received within the *EBSCOhost Research Database*. 'Rank' refers to the level of each journal according to the *Association of Business Schools Academic Journal Quality Guide* (version 4, see Harvey *et al.*, 2010). 'Time' refers to the number of months that have elapsed since each article was published in hardcopy, taking February 2015 as the month against which this is judged. 'Category' is an indicator variable with a value of 1 for articles within the bounded rationality sample and a value of 0 for those within the behavioural economics sample (see the appendices to Chapters 2 and 3 for these).

Following diagnostic testing of the linear regression using the full sample, the outlier articles with 112 and 73 citations, respectively, are removed from the sample in order to enhance the normality of the residuals; the regression is run with robust standard errors (vce(hc3) in Stata) in order to minimise the heteroscedasticity of the residuals; and the log of 'Citations' is adopted as the dependent variable in order to minimise the effects of nonlinearity. The descriptive statistics for this adjusted dataset (which is reported in its entirety in Appendix 4.1) are displayed in Table 4.1.

Running the adjusted regression generates the results in Table 4.2, for which the R-squared value is 0.443.

The regression results demonstrate that both the ranking of the journal and the number of months that have elapsed since the article was published in hardcopy are highly significant: both so at the 1 per cent significance level. The directions of these effects are as one would expect: as both the ranking of the journal in which an article is published and the number of months since it was published in hardcopy increases, the number of citations that the article receives increases. Of particular importance for this chapter, though, is the result regarding the categorisation of articles. The results demonstrate that whether an article is included in the

Table 4.1 Citations analysis: the descriptive statistics

Variable	Observations	Mean value	Standard deviation	Minimum value	Maximum value
logCitations	176	0.981	1.025	0	3.584
Rank	344	2.997	0.758	1	4
Time	344	36.811	24.306	1	117
Category	344	0.733	0.443	0	1

Table 4.2 Citations analysis: the regression results

logCitations	Coefficient	Standard error	t-statistic	P > |t|	95% confidence interval	
α	−1.506	0.350	−4.30***	0.000	−2.198	−0.814
Rank	0.433	0.096	4.51***	0.000	0.243	0.622
Time	0.021	0.003	7.85***	0.000	0.016	0.026
Category	0.105	0.140	0.75	0.456	−0.172	0.382

Note: *** Significant at the 1 per cent level of significance.

behavioural economics literature or in the bounded rationality literature is not significantly important. Works of behavioural economics and bounded rationality are equally cited, once the effects of other important explanatory variables have been controlled.

The results in Table 4.2 are clear. However, there remain weaknesses in the diagnostic tests of this analysis. The residuals are not perfectly aligned to a normal distribution, being slightly skewed downwards, with non-normality being particularly evident within the middle of the distribution; there remains evidence of some non-linearity, and from the Ramsey RESET test of specification error the null hypothesis that there are no omitted variables is rejected. The severity of these weaknesses is limited, though.

Conclusions

The analysis of this chapter has suggested that works of behavioural economics and works of bounded rationality tend to be published in different academic journals. Indeed, a greater proportion of the latter are published in the journals that tend to be most 'respected' within the economics discipline and a greater proportion is also published within the more mathematical and theoretical journals. In terms of the wider academic impacts, though, there is no significant difference between works of behavioural economics and works of bounded rationality, once the effects of other important explanatory variables have been controlled.

Reference

Harvey, C. Kelly, A., Morris, H. and Rowlinson, M. (2010) 'Academic Journal Quality Guide: Version 4', *The Association of Business Schools*, www.associationofbusinessschools.org/sites/default/files/Combined%20Journal%20Guide.pdf.

5 Commonality and differentiation

Examined and evaluated

As the preceding chapters demonstrate, the behavioural economics and bounded rationality literatures have much in common with one another but yet are distinct according to a number of important features. These areas of commonality and differentiation are explored in more detail in this chapter, which employs a simple model of consumer choice as a framework for the discussion.

The decision situation

The first area of common ground between the two literatures is the decision situation they tend to study. Both literatures focus primarily on economic decisions (such as those regarding consumption, production, valuation and exchange) and they do so at the level of choice (the 'lower-order' level in the terminology of Chapter 6). The meaning of this is that models of behavioural economics and bounded rationality tend to examine situations in which a decision-maker faces a number of economic options, from among which he needs to select his preferred choice.

Methodological approaches

Following the first area of commonality above, consider the simple case of a consumer who is required to select a bundle composed of two goods, x and y. The consumer's utility is given by $U = f(x, y)$, where $f'(x) > 0$ and $f''(x) < 0$, and similarly $f'(y) > 0$ and $f''(y) < 0$.

The standard model of rational choice, in this case based on the framework of Hicks and Allen (1934), models the consumer as maximising his utility subject to a budget constraint: $\max f(x, y)$ subject to $c(x, y) = M$, where $c(.)$ is the cost function, giving the cost of the consumption bundle, which is set equal to M, the consumer's available income.

The standard model of rational choice in such situations, the 'theory of value', emerged during the marginal revolution of the second half of the nineteenth century and was summarised in 1890 in Marshall's *Principles* (1920). The concept of marginal utility lies at its heart: a concept that consumers act as though they employ in order to maximise their utility. In his 1892 book, *Mathematical Investigations in the Theory of Value and Prices*, Fisher (2009) suggested the whole theory need only depend on consumers' directions of indifference, an argument that Pareto (1980) extended in his *Manuel* of 1906, demonstrating utility need only be measured in an ordinal, and not cardinal, manner for the theory to work. Hicks and Allen (1934) developed this assertion further still, casting the theory of value in the form in which it exists today (indifference curve analysis) and thereby completing the divergence of economics from its previous psychological foundations (Bruni and Sugden, 2007).

The framework of Hicks and Allen (1934) is remarkably elegant, establishing the theory of value on three concepts:

1   The marginal rate of substitution between any two products, defined as 'the quantity of good Y which would just compensate him [the consumer] for the loss of a marginal unit of X' (Hicks and Allen, 1934: 55).
2   Increasing marginal rate of substitution: 'the more we substitute Y for X, the greater will be the marginal rate of substitution of Y for X' (Hicks and Allen, 1934: 57).
3   The ratio of prices between the products.

Geometrically, the first two of these assumptions are represented by indifference curves that are convex to the origin, while the third is represented by a downward-sloping budget line, with a gradient that reflects the price ratio. Combining these concepts leads immediately to the identification of the consumption bundle that maximises the consumer's utility:

> If the individual is to be in equilibrium with respect to a system of market prices, his marginal rate of substitution between any two goods must equal the ratio of their prices. Otherwise he would clearly find an advantage in substituting some quantity of one for an equal value (at the market rate) of the other.
>
> (Hicks and Allen, 1934: 56)

Geometrically, then, the optimal consumption bundle is that at which there is tangency between the budget line and an indifference curve (see Figure 5.1).

Methodological approaches of bounded rationality

Three general methodological approaches are adopted in works of bounded rationality, the most prevalent being the imposition of additional constraints on a decision-maker who makes decisions through utility optimisation (although it is commonly asserted in the literature that the approach of bounded rationality does not assume optimisation but maintains the standard assumptions regarding a decision-maker's preferences; for example, see Crawford, 2013). As discussed in Chapter 3 (and examined in Mallard, 2012), such additional constraints have taken one of at least three distinct forms. The first is that of constraining the consumer's

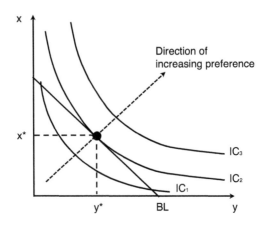

Figure 5.1 Standard utility maximisation

information. For example, in the works of Mackowiak and Wiederholt (2012), Matejka and McKay (2012) and Chen and Zhang (2011), the decision-maker is required to acquire relevant information but doing so is costly and so the decision-maker has to balance the benefit of gaining further information with the cost of doing so. The second involves constraining the ability of the consumer to process the information available to him, either because of the nature of the decision-making processor he has available (such as in Salant, 2011; Halpern and Pass, 2015; and the quantal response models of Rogers *et al.*, 2009, and Le Coq and Sturluson, 2013) or because of the cost of processing the information (for example, as in Tutino, 2013). The third imposes constraints on the range of responses from among which the consumer is able to select, as in Eliaz and Rubinstein (2014), Eliaz and Spiegler (2011) and Glazer and Rubinstein (2012), for example. Each of these approaches can be viewed as restricting the range of possible options ultimately available to the consumer, which is shown in Figure 5.2 by the shaded bundle set. By maximising utility subject to such additional constraints, the consumer's choice may be distorted from that of the standard model of rational choice: to bundle (x_1, y_1) rather than (x^*, y^*).

The second methodological approach to modelling bounded rationality, that remaining true to the intentions of the originator of bounded rationality (Herbert Simon), is that of satisficing. Simon (1955) suggests a model of satisficing in which the consumer establishes minimum aspired quantities of both goods x and y: the minimum physical quantities of the goods that characterise a satisfactory bundle for the consumer. These are denoted by x_{min} and y_{min} in Figure 5.3. The bundles that the consumer deems satisfactory in this case, then, are those contained in the set bounded below by x_{min} and y_{min}. Given the consumer's budget constraint (reflected by the budget line), the satisfactory consumption set available to the consumer is shown by the shaded triangle, with the emboldened section of the budget line representing the satisfactory bundles that perfectly exhaust the consumer's income.

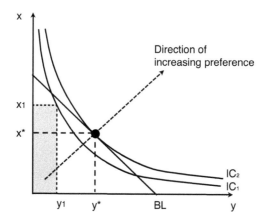

Figure 5.2 Additional constraints

However, models within the bounded rationality literature tend to assume the consumer establishes minimum aspired utilities rather than physical quantities (see, for example, the quantal response equilibrium model of Chen *et al.*, 1997, and the works on savings behaviour and monetary policy by Binswanger, 2010, 2012).

The final methodological approach adopted in the bounded rationality literature is that of heuristic-governed decision-making: modelling the consumer as employing simplifying rules of thumb to actually make his choice. This approach is less concerned with identifying the consumption set from among which the consumer will select his chosen bundle (which collapses to a single, specific bundle in the case of constrained optimisation) and more concerned with the choice process that the consumer employs. As such, the heuristic-governed approach is

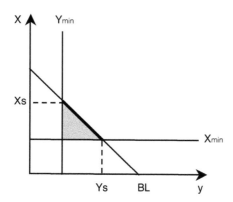

Figure 5.3 Satisficing

compatible with that promoted in the algorithmic social science and computable economics literatures (see Velupillai, 2000, 2010), the proponents of which argue that being able to identify the precise process by which an economic decision is made is essential in order to assure that a consumption choice not only exists but is achievable by human decision-makers in real time. Such an approach has been employed in the work of Manzini and Mariotti (2007) and Sordi and Vercelli (2012), the latter in the form of simple rules of expectations formation.

Methodological approaches of behavioural economics

There are also at least three discernible methodological approaches that have been adopted within the behavioural economics literature. The first is that of examining the decision-maker's precise preferences in different decision situations: personal preferences regarding choices with immediate payoffs (such as in the work of Tonin and Vlassopoulos, 2013), personal preferences regarding choices with future payoffs (for example, in Brown *et al.*, 2009, and Sloan *et al.*, 2014) and also pro-social preferences (as in the work on cooperation by Vanberg, 2008; Volk *et al.*, 2012; and Bigoni *et al.*, 2013). In terms of the simple model of consumer choice running through this section, these can be seen to be endowing the consumer with a utility function of the form $U = f(\alpha x, \beta y)$, where the values of α and β then become the point of focus.

The second approach involves examining the effects that external, 'non-economic' information have on the decision-maker's choice, where such information is defined as information that according to the standard model of economic rationality should not influence the final choice at all. This primarily involves the way in which options are presented to the consumer, such as in List and Samek (2015), McCluskey *et al.* (2011) and Chandler and Kapelner (2013). In terms of the simple model of this section, then, these works can be seen as assuming the consumer possesses a utility function of the form $U = f(x, y, \epsilon)$, where ϵ represents this additional information. Changes in this information, such as the way in which the available options are presented to the decision-maker (expressing them in terms that relate to losses or to gains, for instance) or the order in which they are revealed to the decision-maker, can be seen as manipulating the decision-maker's preferences and so altering the positioning of the decision-maker's indifference curves. Consider Figure 5.4, in which changing the information has shifted the decision-maker's indifference curves from map A to map B, causing the direction of increasing preference to change from D_A to D_B and the bundle chosen to be (x^*_B, y^*_B) rather than (x^*_A, y^*_A).

The third approach is that of examining the actual processes involved in economic decision-making. The works on the effects of anchoring can be included here, such as those of McAlvanah and Moul (2013), Bucchianeri and Minson (2013) and Corrigan *et al.* (2014). Further examples include Rubinstein (2007) and Dickhaut *et al.* (2013) into the different response times of decision-makers. As with the heuristics-governed approach within the bounded rationality literature, such works are more concerned with the actual processes that the consumer

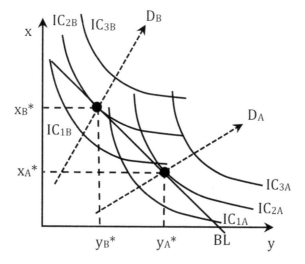

Figure 5.4 Non-economic information

employs to make his selection than with identifying the consumption set from which the choice is made.

Complementarity of the methodological approaches

These methodological approaches employed within the two literatures are complementary: perhaps most clearly evidenced by the fact that they can be illustrated through a common, and simple, model of decision-making such as that examined above. It becomes clear from the discussion above that the two literatures both examine decision-making at the level of choice but that they do so in different ways. Works of bounded rationality, tending to take preference functions as given, examine the effects of decision-making in situations in which the decision-maker is cognitively unable to make a choice as if according to the standard model of rational choice: decision-making that is modelled through approximations based on behavioural observations rather than on fully descriptive behaviour. As Glazer and Rubinstein (2012: 1076) comment, 'We obviously do not view the bounded rationality element in our model as an exact description of reality. Nevertheless, we believe that it captures some elements of real life'. This is representative of the field. Behavioural economics, by contrast, is concerned about the precise psychological drivers that lie beneath decision-making.

Research methods

The discussion in the previous section focuses on the general methodological approaches employed within the bounded rationality and behavioural economics literatures. There are also clear lines of distinction between the specific research methods employed in the two literatures, which are evident from the literature reviews presented in Chapters 2 and 3.

Many of the 'behavioural traits' papers within the behavioural economics literature employ experimental methods, of a range of different types. Charness *et al.* (2013) present a survey of these methods, suggesting that the new category of 'extra-laboratory experiments' should be added to the usual categories of laboratory and field experiments (see Harrison and List, 2004, for a survey of the latter). All three of these are evident within the behavioural economics literature.

1   *Laboratory experiments* are controlled scenarios in which subjects respond to predetermined information or to the actions of others, usually conducted on university students in laboratories on university campuses. For example, Arunachalam *et al.* (2009) employ such research methods to test the finding that increasing the number of options available to consumers causes the overall amount of consumption to fall (the 'excessive-choice effect'); and Slonim *et al.* (2013) conduct such experiments in order to test the strength of the assertion that the usual type of subjects in economics experiments (students in western universities) are not representative of the population as a whole (see Levitt and List, 2007a, 2007b), finding that this criticism may indeed be valid.

2   *Field experiments* are controlled scenarios in which subjects respond to predetermined information or to the actions of others, conducted outside of university campuses on specific, non-student subjects who are unaware that they are being studied (following the definition of Charness *et al.*, 2013). Examples of these include the study of Chandler and Kapelner (2013), in which workers from Amazon's *Mechanical Turk* (an online labour market) are subjected to a field experiment examining the effects on their motivation levels of framing their tasks in different ways; and that of Bucciol *et al.* (2011), which subjects young children to the temptation of eating an unhealthy snack in order to examine whether or not their subsequent productivity in a creative task is impaired by having performed this act of self-control.

3   *Extra-laboratory experiments* are the same as field experiments, with the exception that the subjects in extra-laboratory experiments are aware that they are being studied (again, following the definition of Charness *et al.*, 2013). For example, D'Exelle and van den Berg (2014) experimentally study the effects on aid distribution and cooperation caused by the presence of a group representative in a field laboratory in Nicaragua; and Barham *et al.* (2014) employ a similar approach to test for the effects of risk and ambiguity aversion on the adoption of genetic modification technology by farmers in two US states.

In addition to these, there are also papers that employ a fourth type of experimental method: *online experiments* (scenarios uploaded to the internet, to which subjects are required to respond). Examples of these include Oechssler *et al.* (2009), which investigates the relationship between a person's cognitive ability and the behavioural biases that they exhibit; and Rubinstein (2007), which examines the response times of students when solving problems in game theory.

As well as conducting economic experiments, works within the behavioural economics literature take advantage of existing empirical datasets, analysing them statistically to identify significant relationships between variables; and they also analyse theoretically the effects of more realistic behavioural assumptions on decision-making. Adopting the first of these methods are the papers by Pirinsky (2013) and Cornelissen *et al.* (2013); the first of which analyses data from the *World Values Survey* to study how people's confidence relates to their attitudes towards entrepreneurship, competition and cooperation (and how these relationships vary across cultures), while the second analyses household data from the *German Socio-Economic Panel* to investigate the relationship between workers' feelings of unfairness about the tax system and their rates of absenteeism from work. Examples of the theoretical approach in the behavioural economics literature include Dietl *et al.* (2013), which analyses a principal-agent model to shed light on the effects of taxing bonuses on the behaviour of both parties; and Gürtler and Gürtler (2012), which assesses the effects of inequality aversion on players' behaviour within a general game theory setting.

The bounded rationality literature is much more one dimensional in terms of the research methods it employs than that of behavioural economics: it largely adopts the theoretical approach. As Rubinstein (2007: 1243) asserts, the bounded rationality approach primarily uses 'casual observations of the way in which people make decisions… to construct abstract models which are intended to increase our understanding of the effect of certain decision-procedural elements on the outcome of an economic interaction'. However, this is not to say that the literature is devoid of non-mathematical research methods. For example, Burton and Rigby (2012) and Reise *et al.* (2012) both analyse survey data; the former to examine whether or not individuals voluntarily choose to increase the complexity of the tasks they face within a discrete choice experiment (in which they find that 30 per cent of respondents choose the most demanding tasks), and in the latter to investigate the investment behaviour of German farmers regarding renewable energy systems (from which they find that the farmers' subjective perception of risk and their inability to fully process relevant information are both important). Kalayci and Potters (2011), by contrast, conduct a laboratory experiment, in which sellers choose the number of attributes of their goods that they announce to consumers, in order to examine the effects of increasing consumer confusion (represented by increasing the number of attributes announced). They find that consumers make more suboptimal choices as their level of confusion rises. As a final example, Crawford and Iriberri (2007) analyse empirical data generated by previous experiments (a meta-analysis) in order to explain both the winner's curse in common-value auctions and overbidding in independent private-value auctions.

Focus and fields of application

Both the literatures of bounded rationality and behavioural economics are concerned with decision-making that is suboptimal from the perspective of the standard model of rational choice. However, the focus of the bounded rationality literature tends not to be on the decision-making *per se* but on the theoretical effects that such decision-making has on the wider economic situation, while the focus of behavioural economics tends to be on actual decision-making processes and on the psychological fundamentals that underpin them. Perhaps emanating directly from this division of focus is the breadth of the applications of the two approaches.

As Chapter 3 outlines, the bounded rationality approach has been applied to situations of standard choice, uncertain choice, inter-temporal choice, strategic choice and macroeconomic behaviour. Although these applications focus on a range of specific situations, such as the market for charlatan medical practitioners (Spiegler, 2006), the choice of travel route (Chorus *et al.*, 2006), electoral voting (Osborne and Rubinstein, 2003) and the choice of environmental policy (Stranlund and Ben-Haim, 2008), the focus tends to be on the theoretical effects of suboptimal decision-making rather than on the application itself.

Similar is also true of the 'behavioural traits' works in behavioural economics (outlined in Chapter 2), which adopt the primary focus of generating further insights into the preferences, actual processes, 'non-economic' information and decision fatigue involved in economic decision-making (along with how such decision-making can be manipulated). However, the behavioural economics literature also consists of a burgeoning array of 'application' papers that further develop and test the findings of the categories of papers above in a whole array of different situations, such as the study behaviour of undergraduate students (Delaney *et al.*, 2013), the behaviour of juries (Baddeley and Parkinson, 2013) and the motivation of non-profit organisations (Bengtsson and Engstrom, 2013). Furthermore, the behavioural economics literature also consists of an equally voluminous (at least) range of 'suggestive' survey articles, which each propose how existing findings within the literature can be applied to new fields of study. For example, such surveys have drawn on the behavioural economics literature to propose programmes of future study related to the economics of climate-change (Brekke and Johansson-Stenmann, 2008; Gowdy, 2008), financial literacy (Altman, 2012), travel demand modelling (Avineri, 2012) and the design and implementation of development policies (Datta and Mullainathan, 2014). Contributions such as these are unique within economics to the literature of behavioural economics.

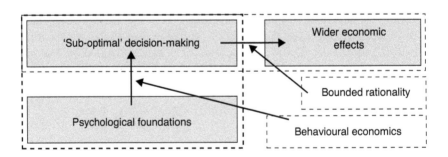

Figure 5.5 Focus of bounded rationality and behavioural economics

Analytical power

The goal to which economists strive is the development of models and theories characterised by maximum analytical power (defined as the degree to which a model's usefulness exceeds its level of descriptive detail). A model that is perfectly descriptive (and so not at all parsimonious) is of maximum usefulness in the specific situation being studied, but is unlikely to be applicable in situations beyond that, thereby having little analytical power overall. Conversely, a model that is perfectly parsimonious (and so not accurately descriptive at all) is unlikely to be applicable or useful in any situation, giving it even less analytical power. The goal, therefore, is to develop a model or theory that is characterised by the level of descriptive detail at which the marginal benefit of detail (TB'_D) is equal to the marginal cost of detail (TC'_D), where $TB'_D > 0$, $TB''_D < 0$, $TC'_D > 0$ and $TC''_D > 0$. In Figure 5.6, this is the point D^*.

As a result of their different focuses of study, with works of behavioural economics examining the precise nature of preferences and decision-making processes while those of bounded rationality tending to assume these are given, the two literatures operate at different degrees of detail/parsimony. The bounded rationality and behavioural economics approaches have evolved along different paths in terms of drawing the line between behavioural realism on the one hand and model simplicity and range of applicability on the other (see Augier and March, 2008). The former draws the line at greater parsimony (particularly in works that maintain the assumption of optimisation at the lower-order level of choice), striking the balance at D_{BR} in Figure 5.6; whereas the latter draws the line at greater behavioural realism and descriptive detail, examining preferences and decision-making processes in specific situations (albeit maintaining the optimisation procedure of choice in many cases; see Crawford, 2013), striking the balance at D_{BE} instead.

Discussion

It is evident from this chapter that the literatures of behavioural economics and bounded rationality have evolved along different paths, even though they both have their origins in discontentment with the standard model of rational choice as a descriptive and predictive model of economic decision-making (manifested in the works of Daniel Kahneman and Amos Tversky, and of Herbert Simon, respectively). The literatures are both concerned with economic decision-making at the lower-order level of choice, but they focus on different aspects of this: bounded rationality on the wider economic effects of decision-making that is suboptimal from the perspective of the standard model of economic rationality because decision-makers are cognitively unable to fully deal with the complexity of the decisions; and behavioural economics on people's preferences and the actual processes and influences involved in such decision-making. Perhaps as a direct result of these differences in focus, the literatures have evolved different methodologies. That of bounded rationality primarily involves the theoretical analysis of assumed and abstract decision-making procedures (based on 'casual observations'

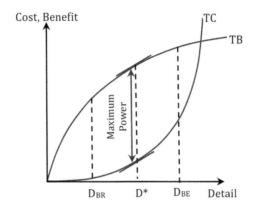

Figure 5.6 The detail/parsimony balance

of actual behaviour – Rubinstein, 2007: 1243) intended to approximate behaviour in situations when the decision-maker is cognitively not up to the task of acting as if in accordance to the standard model of rational choice. That of behavioural economics, by contrast, largely involves the use of an increasingly wide range of experimental methods to deepen our understanding of actual decision-making processes.

The first argument that should be made here arises naturally from consideration of David Ricardo's theory of comparative advantage. The two literatures have largely been driven forward by different academics: the bounded rationality literature primarily by academics schooled in economics and the behavioural economics literature primarily by those schooled in psychology. It is unsurprising, then, that the literatures possess their different focuses and that works of bounded rationality tend to keep the black box of preferences and cognitive processes shut while the investigative works of behavioural economics tend to leave the wider economic effects unexamined (which has led to the burgeoning literature of suggestive survey articles that has emerged to fill this gap; see Chapter 2). Arguably, this is precisely how it should be, as it reflects specialisation according to lines of comparative advantage, enlarging the subsequent production of findings and developments to the benefit of all involved. Indeed, it would be wasteful for academic economists (and psychologists) to retrain as psychologists (economists) in order that a common path be pursued. It would also be infeasible in an academic environment in which participants are judged according to the volume and academic quality of their research output; and in which those who determine the quality of a given piece of academic research (the editors of academic journals in each discipline) naturally tend to favour the research methods traditionally employed in their respective disciplines.

The methodological pluralism that has emerged because of the contrasting paths taken by the bounded rationality and behavioural economics literatures, and the ever-widening scope of the fields and issues they examine, has certainly enriched the subject of economics as a whole. The number of students who have decided to pursue economics degree courses largely on the basis of having read books such as *Predictably Irrational* (Ariely, 2009) and *Nudge* (Thaler and Sunstein, 2009) (the 'Ariely effect') and being interested in the processes of economic decision-making (and how we do not act in perfect accordance with *homo economicus*) should not be underestimated. Neither should the effect that behavioural economics has had on making economics accessible to those not interested in abstract, mathematical modelling. Indeed, the growth of behavioural economics has revitalised the relevance of economics as a whole, which has been particularly important in the wake of the financial crisis of 2008 and the resulting discon-tentment with the efficacy of the discipline.

The separate evolution of the two literatures has also resulted in an abundance of information that is directly relevant for policy-making, in a whole array of situations. The behavioural economics literature is replete with studies that directly and explicitly examine the design and implementation of policies. At the level of individual behaviour, for example, List and Samek (2015) and McCluskey *et al.* (2011) both examine ways in which children can be induced to have healthier diets. More specifically, the former finds little effect of framing incentives differently: as positive incentives (meaning the children are rewarded for eating more healthily) or as negative incentives (meaning that they lose their reward if they do not eat more healthily); while the second finds that children can be induced to eat more healthily through changes to the design of menus. And at the level of policies for society as a whole, for example, are the studies of Brekke and Johansson-Stenmann (2008) and Gowdy (2008) into the design of climate change policies, and Datta and Mullainathan (2014) into similar issues relating to development policies. Indeed, behavioural economics has lead to the whole policy approach of libertarian paternalism (the 'Nudge approach': see Thaler and Sunstein, 2009) and the resulting debate regarding its ethical and practical implications. In the UK, for instance, the Behavioural Insights Team was established as the first government institution specifically dedicated to the application of behavioural economics to public policy and it continues to produce research that directly informs public policy. The bounded rationality literature is undeniably concerned with policy as well, but in the more abstract and less informative manner that arises naturally from its methodological approach. For example, Spiegler (2006) demonstrates in a study of the market for 'quacks' (charlatan medical practitioners) in which the information available to patients is constrained to that from anecdotal reasoning of random, casual stories regarding the quality of treatments (based on the S(1) procedure of Osborne and Rubinstein, 1998; namely, patients identifying whether each of the treatments of which they are aware – either from personal experience or from anecdotes from other patients – was a success or a failure, and then choosing the optimal alternative from that set) that unless the quality of patients' reasoning is raised above the anecdotal level, ordinary competition policies may be ineffective. As such, this swell of policy relevance would not have occurred had just the more traditional economics approach embodied in the bounded rationality literature been pursued.

However, both literatures have been exposed to criticism. The fundamental criticism that is levelled at the literatures is that they have not yet succeeded in presenting a single and coherent alternative model to the standard model of rational choice. Instead, they have generated an impressive array of different decision-making processes (both theoretical and from observations of actual behaviour). Without an accompanying framework as to which particular process is relevant in which decision situation, though, works based on behavioural assumptions can be seen as starting from rather arbitrary and *ad hoc* foundations. That this criticism bears much weight in the literature is evident from the following quotations:

1   '[W]hat is still lacking [with bounded rationality and behavioural economics] is a body of systematic theory that is as orderly and teachable as the neoclassical theory of the firm' (Harstad and Selten, 2013: 498).
2   '[T]hose who advocate bounded rationality modeling must find comparably convincing, evidence-based ways to choose among the equally enormous number of possible non-optimizing models' (Crawford, 2013: 524).
3   'Our reading of the literature suggests that even papers that find evidence consistent with one interpretation are often unable to rule out other mechanisms that are also consistent with their results' (Astebro *et al.*, 2014: 51).
4   'Under certain circumstances [behavioural economics has demonstrated that] people indeed CAN and often DO deviate from rational choice assumptions. What it does not show is that people are by nature predictably irrational' (Rona-Tas and Guseva, 2013: 421–422).

There has been progress in the literature towards addressing this criticism. This has taken the form both of new models that seek to establish an overarching model of decision-making (the 'top-down approach', such as that by Bernheim and Rangel, 2009) and also that of demonstrating the relationships between existing models of decision-making, thereby moving the literature naturally towards a common, unified framework (such as that of Miettinen, 2009, which demonstrates the link between the partially cursed equilibrium of Eyster and Rabin, 2005, and the analogy-based expectation equilibrium of Jehiel and Koessler, 2007 – the 'botton-up approach'). However, this is the single most important area in which the literatures would benefit from coming together and informing the evolution of one another: harnessing the progress being made in the theoretical modelling of behaviour and in our understanding of the processes and influences involved. Presenting a possible avenue for such collaboration is the focus of the next chapter.

References

Altman, M. (2012) 'Implications of behavioural economics for financial literacy and public policy', *Journal of Socio-Economics* 41, 677–690.

Ariely, D. (2009) *Predictably Irrational: The Hidden Forces that Shape Our Decisions*, London: Harper-Collins.

Arunachalam, B., Henneberry, S.R., Lusk, J.L. and Bailey Norwood, F. (2009) 'An empirical investigation into the excessive-choice effect', *American Journal of Agricultural Economics* 91, 810–825.

Astebro, T., Herz, H., Nanda, R. and Weber, R.A. (2014) 'Seeking the roots of entrepreneurship: insights from behavioral economics', *Journal of Economic Perspectives* 28, 49–70.

Augier, M. and March, J.G. (2008), 'Realism and comprehension in economics: a footnote to an exchange between Oliver E. Williamson and Herbert A. Simon', *Journal of Economic Behavior & Organization* 66, 95–105.

Avineri, E. (2012) 'On the use and potential of behavioural economics from the perspective of transport and climate change', *Journal of Transport Geography* 24, 512–521.

Baddeley, M. and Parkinson, S. (2012), 'Group decision-making: an economic analysis of social influence and individual difference in experimental juries', *Journal of Socio-Economics* 41, 558–573.

Barham, B.L., Chavas, J.-P., Fitz, D., Rios Salas, V. and Schechter, L. (2014) 'The roles of risk and ambiguity in technology adoption', *Journal of Economic Behavior & Organization* 97, 204–218.

Bengtsson, N. and Engstrom, P. (2013), 'Replacing trust with control: a field test of motivation crowd out theory', *Economic Journal* 124, 833–858.

Bernheim, D. and Rangel A. (2009) 'Beyond revealed preference: choice-theoretic foundations for behavioral welfare economics', *Quarterly Journal of Economics* 124, 51–105.

Bigoni, M., Camera, G. and Casari, M. (2013) 'Strategies of cooperation and punishment among students and clerical workers', *Journal of Economic Behavior & Organization* 94, 172–182.

Binswanger, J. (2010) 'Understanding the heterogeneity of savings and asset allocation: a behavioral-economics perspective', *Journal of Economic Behavior & Organization* 76, 296–317.

Binswanger, J. (2012) 'Life cycle saving: insights from the perspective of bounded rationality', *European Economic Review* 56, 605–623.

Brekke, K.A. and Johansson-Stenman, O. (2008) 'The behavioural economics of climate change', *Oxford Review of Economic Policy* 24, 280–297.

Brown, A.L., Chua, Z.E. and Camerer, C.F. (2009) 'Learning and visceral temptation in dynamic saving experiments', *Quarterly Journal of Economics* 124, 197–231.

Bruni, L. and Sugden, R. (2007) 'The road not taken: how psychology was removed from economics, and how it might be brought back', *Economic Journal* 117, 146–173.

Bucchianeri, G.W. and Minson, J.A. (2013) 'A homeowner's dilemma: anchoring in residential real estate transactions', *Journal of Economic Behavior & Organization* 89, 76–92.

Bucciol, A., Houser, D. and Piovesan, M. (2011) 'Temptation and productivity: a field experiment with children', *Journal of Economic Behavior & Organization* 78, 126–136.

Burton, M. and Rigby, D. (2012) 'The self selection of complexity in choice experiments', *American Journal of Agricultural Economics* 94, 786–800.

Chandler, D. and Kapelner, A. (2013) 'Breaking monotony with meaning: motivation in crowdsourcing markets', *Journal of Economic Behavior & Organization* 90, 123–133.

Charness, G., Gneezy, U. and Kuhn, M.A. (2013) 'Experimental methods: extra-laboratory experiments – extending the reach of experimental economics', *Journal of Behavior & Organization* 91, 93–100.

Chen, H.-C., J.W. Friedman and Thisse, J.-F. (1997) 'Boundedly rational Nash Equilibrium: a probabilistic choice approach', *Games & Economic Behavior* 18, 32–54.

Chen, Y. and Zhang, T. (2011) 'Equilibrium price dispersion with heterogeneous searchers', *International Journal of Industrial Organization* 29, 645–654.

Chorus, C.G., T.A. Arentze, E.J.E. Molin, H.J.P. Timmermans and Van Wee, B. (2006) 'The value of travel information: decision strategy-specific conceptualizations and numerical examples', *Transportation Research Part B* 40, 504–519.

Cornelissen, T., Himmler, O. and Koenig, T. (2013) 'Fairness spillovers – the case of taxation', *Journal of Economic Behavior & Organization* 90, 164–180.

Corrigan, J.R., Rousu, M.C. and Depositario, D.P.T. (2014) 'Do practice rounds affect experimental auction results?' *Economic Letters* 123, 42–44.

Crawford, V.P. (2013) 'Boundedly rational versus optimization-based models of strategic thinking and learning in games', *Journal of Economic Literature* 51, 512–527.

Crawford, V.P. and Iriberri, N. (2007) 'Level-k auctions: can a nonequilibrium model of strategic thinking explain the winner's curse and overbidding in private-value auctions?' *Econometrica* 75, 1721–1770.

Datta, S. and Mullainathan, S. (2014) 'Behavioral design: a new approach to development policy', *Review of Income and Wealth* 60, 7–36.

Delaney, L., Harmon, C. and Ryan, M. (2013) 'The role of noncognitive traits in undergraduate study behaviours', *Economics of Education Review* 32, 181–195.

D'Exelle, B. and van den Berg, M. (2014) 'Aid distribution and cooperation in unequal communities', *Review of Income & Wealth* 60, 114–132.

Dickhaut, J., Smith, V., Xin, B. and Rustichini, A. (2013) 'Human economic choice as costly information processing', *Journal of Economic Behavior & Organization* 94, 206–221.

Dietl, H.M., Grossman, M., Lang, M. and Wey, S. (2013) 'Incentive effects of bonus taxes in a principal-agent model', *Journal of Economic Behavior & Organization* 89, 93–104.

Eliaz, K. and Rubinstein, A. (2014) 'A model of boundedly rational "neuro" agents', *Economic Theory* 57, 515–528.

Eliaz, K. and Spiegler, R. (2011) 'Consideration sets and competitive marketing', *Review of Economic Studies* 78, 235–262.

Eyster, E. and Rabin, M. (2005) 'Cursed equilibrium', *Econometrica* 73, 1623–1672.

Fisher, I. (2009) *Mathematical Investigations in the Theory of Value and Price*, Montana, USA: Kessinger Publishing.

Glazer, J. and Rubinstein, A. (2012) 'A model of persuasion with boundedly rational agents', *Journal of Political Economy* 120, 1057–1082.

Gowdy, J.M. (2008) 'Behavioral economics and climate change policy', *Journal of Economic Behavior & Organization* 68, 632–644.

Gürtler, M. and Gürtler, O. (2012) 'Inequality aversion and externalities', *Journal of Economic Behavior & Organization* 84, 111–117.

Halpern, J.Y. and Pass, R. (2015) 'Algorithmic rationality: game theory with costly computation', *Journal of Economic Theory* 156, 246–268.

Harrison, G.W. and List, J.A. (2004) 'Field experiments', *Journal of Economic Literature* 42, 1009–1055.

Harstad, R.M. and Selten, R. (2013) 'Bounded-rationality models: tasks to become intellectually competitive', *Journal of Economic Literature* 51, 496–511.

Hicks, J.R. and Allen, R.G.D. (1934) 'A reconsideration of the theory of value, part 1', *Economica* 1, 52–76.

Jehiel, P. and Koessler, F. (2007) 'Revisiting games of incomplete information with analogy based expectations', *Games & Economic Behavior* 62, 533–557.

Kalayci, K. and Potters, J. (2011) 'Buyer confusion and market prices', *International Journal of Industrial Organization* 29, 14–22.

Le Coq, C. and Sturluson, J.T. (2013) 'Does opponents' experience matter? Experimental evidence from a quantity precommitment game', *Journal of Economic Behavior & Organization* 84, 265–277.

Levitt, S.D. and List, J.A. (2007a) 'What do laboratory experiments measuring social preferences reveal about the real world?' *Journal of Economic Perspectives* 21, 153–174.

Levitt, S.D. and List, J.A. (2007b) 'Viewpoint: on the generalizability of lab behaviour to the field', *Canadian Journal of Economics* 40, 347–370.

List, J.A. and Samek, A.S. (2015) 'The behavioralist as nutritionist: leveraging behavioral economics to improve child food choice and consumption', *Journal of Health Economics* 39, 135–146.

Mackowiak, B. and Wiederholt, M. (2012) 'Information processing and limited liability', *American Economic Review Papers and Proceedings* 102, 30–34.

Mallard, G. (2012) 'Modelling cognitively bounded rationality: an evaluative taxonomy', *Journal of Economic Surveys* 26, 674–704.

Manzini, P. and Mariotti, M. (2007) 'Sequentially rationalizable choice', *American Economic Review* 97, 1824–1839.

Marshall, A. (1920) *Principles of Economics*, Volume 1, Eighth Edition, London: Macmillan.

Matejka, F. and McKay, A. (2012) 'Simple market equilibria with rationally inattentive consumers', *American Economic Review Papers and Proceedings* 102, 24–29.

McAlvanah, P. and Moul, C.C. (2013) 'The house doesn't always win: evidence of anchoring among Australian bookies', *Journal of Economic Behavior & Organization* 90, 87–99.

McCluskey, J.J., Mittelhammer, R.C. and Asiseh, F. (2011) 'From default to choice: adding healthy options to kids' menus', *American Journal of Agricultural Economics* 94, 338–343.

Miettinen, T. (2009) 'The partially cursed and the analogy-based expectation equilibrium', *Economics Letters* 105, 162–164.

Oechssler, J., Roider, A. and Schmitz, P.W. (2009) 'Cognitive abilities and behavioral biases', *Journal of Economic Behavior & Organization* 72, 147–152.

Osbourne, M. and Rubinstein, A. (1998) 'Games with procedurally rational players', *American Economic Review* 88, 834–849.

Osbourne, M. and Rubinstein, A. (2003) 'Sampling equilibrium, with an application to strategic voting', *Games & Economic Behavior* 45, 434–441.

Pareto, V. (1980) *Manuel of Political Economy*, Reprint Edition, USA: Kelley.

Pirinsky, C. (2013) 'Confidence and economic attitudes', *Journal of Behavior & Organization* 91, 139–158.

Reise, C., Musshoff, O., Granoszewski, K. and Spiller, A. (2012) 'Which factors influence the expansion of bioenergy? An empirical study of the investment behaviours of German farmers', *Ecological Economics* 73, 133–141.

Rogers, B.W., Palfrey, T.R. and Camerer, C.F. (2009) 'Heterogeneous quantal response equilibrium and cognitive hierarchies', *Journal of Economic Theory* 144, 1440–1467.

Rona-Tas, A. and Guseva, A. (2013) 'Information and consumer credit in Central and Eastern Europe', *Journal of Comparative Economics* 41, 420–435.

Rubinstein, A. (2007) 'Instinctive and cognitive reasoning: a study of response times', *Economic Journal* 117, 1243–1259.

Salant, Y. (2011) 'Procedural analysis of choice rules with applications to bounded rationality', *American Economic Review* 101(2), 724–748.

Sloan, F.A., Eldred, L.M. and Xu, Y. (2014) 'The behavioral economics of drunk driving', *Journal of Health Economics* 35, 64–81.

Slonim, R., Wang, C., Garbarino, E. and Merrett, D. (2013) 'Opting-in: participation bias in economic experiments', *Journal of Economic Behavior & Organization* 90, 43–47.

Sordi, S. and Vercelli, A. (2012) 'Heterogeneous expectations and strong uncertainty in a Minskyian model of financial fluctuations' *Journal of Economic Behavior & Organization* 83, 544–557.

Spiegler, R. (2006) 'The market for quacks', *Review of Economic Studies* 73, 1113–1131.

Simon, H.A. (1955) 'A behavioural model of rational choice', *Quarterly Journal of Economics* 69, 99–118.

Stranlund, J.K. and Ben-Haim, Y. (2008) 'Price-based vs. quantity-based environmental regulation under Knightian uncertainty: an info-gap robust satisficing perspective', *Journal of Environmental Management* 87, 443–449.

Thaler, R.H. and Sunstein, C.R. (2009) *Nudge: Improving Decisions about Health, Wealth and Happiness*, New York: Penguin.

Tonin, M. and Vlassopoulos, M. (2013) 'Experimental evidence of self-image concerns as motivation for giving', *Journal of Economic Behavior & Organization* 90, 19–27.

Tutino, A. (2013) 'Rationally inattentive consumption choice', *Review of Economic Dynamics* 16, 421–439.

Vanberg, C. (2008) 'Why do people keep their promises? An experimental test of two explanations', *Econometrica* 76, 1467–1480.

Volk, S., Thoni, C. and Ruigrok, W. (2012) 'Temporal stability and psychological foundations of cooperation preferences', *Journal of Economic Behavior & Organziation* 81, 664–676.

Velupillai, K.V. (2000) *Computable Economics: The Arne Ryde Memorial Lectures*, Oxford, UK: Oxford University Press.

Velupillai, K.V. (2010) *Computable Foundations for Economics: Methodology and Philosophy*, Abingdon, UK: Routledge.

6 Towards an abstract behavioural framework

The fundamental criticism levelled at the behavioural economics and bounded rationality literatures is that neither has succeeded in presenting a general, abstract framework of economic decision-making that can replace the standard model of rational choice. In terms of Figure 5.6, this criticism asserts that the analytical power of these literatures remains less than that of the model of standard economic rationality. Indeed, the fundamental criticism of these literatures is that they have spawned (and continue to spawn) an array of different types of preference functions and decision-making processes, each of which is demonstrably applicable in specific situations and generates interesting findings supported by observed behaviour, but there is no accompanying framework as to which type of preference function or decision-making process is applicable to a new, given situation; a problem that is particular severe in the case of behavioural economics. For example, should a decision-maker be assumed to be subject to loss aversion, the endowment effect, decision fatigue or pro-social preferences? And, more specifically, should a decision-maker in a model of strategic interaction be modelled along the lines of the cognitive hierarchy or the quantal response equilibrium approach? And which heuristic devices should a decision-maker be assumed to employ: the peak-end rule or the heuristics of availability, representativeness or anchoring and adjustment? Immediately this makes any model that starts from foundational behavioural assumptions prone to the criticism of being arbitrary and *ad hoc*. As Spiegler 2011 (page 200) asserts:

> What mutes the ad-hockery criticism in the case of the rational-choice model is the existence of a coherent analytical framework, in which all standard economic models are embedded. A comparable abstract framework is, in my opinion, what is missing the most from the current bounded rationality and behavioral economics literature.

A number of papers within the behavioural economics and bounded rationality literatures have been focused on addressing this criticism. Perhaps the most prominent of these is that of Bernheim and Rangel (2009), which presents an alternative general choice framework that takes account of a wide array of non-rational behaviours observed and reported within behavioural economics. At its heart is the replacement of the standard revealed preference relation with an 'unambiguous choice relation', which in its strict sense is defined as good Y never being chosen if good X is available.

The purpose of this chapter is to present, through a simple model of decision-making, a possible avenue of future research to address this criticism. The approach presented here is based on two elements and it draws together the literatures of behavioural economics and bounded rationality. First, it views decision-making as a two-step process, with the decision-maker allocating his limited cognitive reserve in the first step (the 'higher-order' decision), which then constrains the accuracy of his actual choice in the second step (the 'lower-order' decision). Second, it shifts the focus of analysis from that of identifying the precise option selected in the lower-order decision to that of identifying the degree of optimality with which that option is selected.

This approach is related to the works of Mackowiak and Wiederholt (2012), Tirole (2009) and Dickhaut *et al.* (2013). Each of these examines the behaviour of decision-makers who balance the costs of acquiring and processing information with the resulting quality of their decisions. The first is concerned with the effect of a decision-maker possessing limited liability on the thoroughness of his decision-making, whereas the second examines the particular case of parties engaging in contract negotiation, and the resulting completeness of the contracts agreed. The third, adopting the approach of neuroeconomics, presents and tests a model of the neural processes underlying economic choice behaviour.

Decision fatigue

This approach is predicated on the notion of decision fatigue, and so that is outlined here before the chapter proceeds to the presentation of a model of the higher-order part of the approach and to an example of how this can then inform a model of lower-order decision-making.

Decision-making is costly and so as a result it can be rational in certain situations for decision-makers to not make decisions perfectly. This has been considered within the economics literature for some time (Miravete and Palacios-Huerta, 2014). For example, Stigler and Becker (1977: 82) assert that:

> In order to make a decision one requires information, and the information must be analyzed. The costs of searching for information and of applying the information to a new situation may be such that habit is often a more efficient way to deal with moderate or temporary changes in the environment than would be a full, apparently utility-maximizing decision.

Over recent decades, psychologists and behavioural economists have built up a convincing body of evidence that this notion of decision-making being costly is indeed true. Psychologists refer to the internal part of an individual that is responsible for instigating acts of volition, such as decision-making or self-control, as that individual's 'executive function' (Baumeister *et al.*, 1998). An ever-expanding array of evidence demonstrates that an individual's executive function draws on a limited cognitive resource, and that acts of volition deplete this resource. This in turn can lead to one of three possible outcomes until a person's cognitive resource is replenished through rest.

The first is reduced performance in further acts of volition. Baumeister *et al.* (1994) conclude that much evidence about the failure of self-control fits a model of cognitive resource depletion: a conclusion that is supported by Muraven *et al.* (1998), who demonstrate that consecutive exertions of self-control are charac-terised by deteriorating performance, even if the exertions involve seemingly unrelated actions. Within the economics literature, the work of Bucciol *et al.* (2011) also supports this. These authors demonstrate that after young children have resisted the temptation of eating a snack while left to themselves, their produc-tivity in a simple creative task is significantly impaired.

The second is the avoidance of further decisions. Augenblick and Nicholson (2009), exploiting a natural experiment from American elections, show that if voters are required to make more choices prior to a particular decision, the likeli-hood of them abstaining from that particular decision is increased. Iyengar and Lepper (2000) and Boatwright and Nunes (2001) find that reducing the options available to consumers leads to increased numbers of purchases.

The third is the subsequent employment of satisficing heuristics. Levav *et al.* (2010) demonstrate that German car buyers customising their Audis are more likely to choose default options, and thus spend more money on their cars, if decisions with larger numbers of alternatives are placed at the beginning of the customisation process. Augenblick and Nicholson (2009) and Iyengar and Kamenica (2010) similarly show that decision-makers are more likely to choose simpler but suboptimal options when they are presented with larger sets of options from which to choose; and Kalayci and Potters (2011) find that consumers make more suboptimal choices when the goods available to them have a greater number of attributes (even though those attributes are not relevant to the satisfaction to be gained from the goods).

These are all examples of what has become known in the literature as 'decision fatigue' (see Baumeister and Tierney, 2011). As individuals are required to make more numerous or more complex decisions they deplete their cognitive resource, making it more likely that further decisions will be suboptimal, based on heuristics or avoided altogether. Indeed, Cadena and Keys (2013) present evidence that the reason why one in six undergraduate students choose to turn down the offer of interest-free loans (in effect, turning down a substantial free gift of money from the government) lies in their desire to avoid the increased temptation that having such extra liquidity would bring in the future, thereby reducing the possible effects of decision fatigue they will face.

A model of higher-order decision-making

The situation

Consider the following stylised situation. An individual wakes in the morning feeling re-energised and eager to take advantage of the opportunities afforded to him during the day ahead. His limited cognitive resource is fully replenished. As the day proceeds he finds himself having to make one decision after another. Some of these are simple and routine (what to have for breakfast or what shirt to wear to work, for example) but others are more complex and cognitively demanding (what grade to award to an MSc dissertation, for instance). Gradually, he finds himself cognitively tiring and decreasingly able to focus on making decisions optimally; his cognitive resource is being depleted. He can replenish his resource by taking a rest, although this is not always possible. Some days, he retires to bed relatively alert, having had a psychologically undemanding day, whereas on other days he literally collapses into bed unable to think about further decisions and perhaps having postponed an important decision to a future day: procrastination. The next morning, the cycle repeats itself.

More formally, then, the situation is one in which an individual faces a number of decisions (denoted by $n = 1, \ldots, N$) during the day. He has a limited cognitive resource (denoted by Π) to expend in making them, which can be replenished to some degree during the day if he has a complete break from decision-making. The following simplifying assumptions help to motivate the model:

(A1.1)   Cognitive resources cannot be transferred between days: it is not possible for the individual to 'bank' unused resources for use in future days, nor is it possible to 'borrow' surplus resources from future days.

(A1.2)   The more of the cognitive resource that the individual exhausts while making a particular decision, the closer the result of that particular decision will be to optimality; unless, of course, he is already making the decision optimally, which means further allocations of the cognitive resource is a waste. The implication here is that any resource allocation less than that required for optimisation means the individual employs satisficing behaviour for that particular decision; and the greater the gap between the allocation and that required for optimisation, the further the decision made may be from optimality.

(A1.3)   Once the cognitive resource has been exhausted, all subsequent decisions are avoided unless the resource is replenished through rest.

(A1.4)   The individual is able to postpone the making of a decision until a future day: to engage in procrastination.

(A1.5)   Decisions are completely independent from one another: the allocation of the cognitive resource to one decision has no effect on the required allocation for another to be optimised.

(A1.6)   The higher-order decision regarding how to allocate the cognitive resource across the decisions of the day exhausts a negligible amount of the cognitive resource itself. These decisions are made instinctively (a habitual response) and so do not exert much of a burden on the cognitive resource.

This latter assumption requires further elaboration. The behavioural evidence strongly suggests that individuals do not always make decisions optimally: sometimes they employ heuristics and satisficing that simplify decision-making processes. However, there is only limited evidence regarding how individuals assign their limited cognitive resources to the decisions they face; but the evidence that exists suggests that such higher-order decisions are performed near-optimally. For example, Basov (2006) explains that amateur runners often perform to an almost professional standard at calculating the optimal energy expenditure while running over a given distance: an analogous higher-order decision to that of the model here. The explanation for this is that evolution has shaped humans to be able to perform such tasks in this way. This is the idea of 'ecological rationality' (see Cosmides and Tooby, 1994). As such, and faced with no evidence to the contrary, it is here assumed for mathematical tractability that this allocation is performed optimally.

The individual is required to allocate his cognitive resource carefully across the decisions of the day if he is to make decisions effectively. Doing this involves two separate steps – the stage choice and the temporal choice – although in reality they are made simultaneously.

The stage choice

It is possible to categorise the decisions the individual has to make in a given day into three types. First, there are those that arise as a matter of routine (for example, the choice of clothes to wear and the mode of transport to use to travel to work). Second, there are those that are scheduled specifically for that day (such as those involved in a planned shopping trip or that result from having the car serviced). Finally, there are those that are unexpected (those associated with a surprise visit from a colleague or a student, for instance). This leads to a final simplifying assumption:

(A1.7) From experience of similar days in the past, weighted according to how recent and similar to the present day they were (following the case-based decision theory of Gilboa and Schmeidler, 1995), the individual forms expectations of the following:

    i   The number of routine decisions that will need to be made during a given day (denoted by $n_R = 1, ..., N_R$) and of the extent to which each will deplete the cognitive resource if made optimally (denoted by Ψ_{n_R}).

    ii   The number of non-routine decisions specifically scheduled for that day (denoted by $n_P = 1, ..., N_P$) and of the extent to which each will deplete the cognitive resource if made optimally (denoted by Ψ_{n_P}).

    iii The number of unexpected decisions that will need to be made (denoted by $n_S = 1, ..., N_S$) and of the extent to which each will deplete the cognitive resource if made optimally (denoted by Ψ_{n_S}).

Given these, after each decision the individual possesses an expectation of the aggregate cognitive resource required for all subsequent decisions during the remainder of the day to be made through optimisation, Ψ_A, which is given by equation (6.1), in which x, y and z represent the number of routine, scheduled and random decisions that have already been made during the day, respectively:

$$\Psi_A = \sum_{n_R = x+1}^{N_R} \Psi_{n_R} + \sum_{n_P = y+1}^{N_P} \Psi_{n_P} + \sum_{n_S = z+1}^{N_S} \Psi_{n_S} \tag{6.1}$$

From (A1.2) and (A1.3) there are two sources of possible regret for the individual. The first is from allocating too little of the cognitive resource to a particular decision, thereby foregoing utility from that particular decision while not exhausting the cognitive resource during the day. The second is from exhausting the cognitive resource too quickly and then being forced to make subsequent decisions in a suboptimal manner or avoiding them altogether. These can be thought of as the direct and opportunity costs of decision-making, respectively. Optimally, then, the individual allocates the cognitive resource across expected decisions so the total expected regret from making those decisions is minimised. If $\Psi_A \leq \Pi$, the individual will naturally plan to make every decision optimally, but if $\Psi_A > \Pi$, the individual will necessarily have to economise on his decision-making: to employ satisficing for some decisions or to avoid some decisions altogether.

(A1.8)   The nature of expected regret:
  i   The total expected regret from making a particular decision sub-optimally (TR_{PD}) declines as more of the cognitive resource is allocated to it: $\partial TR_{PD}/\partial \pi_{PD} < 0$, where π_{PD} denotes the amount of the cognitive resource allocated to the particular decision. However, the marginal reduction in TR_{PD} slows as more of the cognitive resource is assigned to it: $\partial^2 TR_{PD}/\partial \pi_{PD^2} < 0$, following the law of diminishing marginal returns.
  ii   The total expected regret from making the remaining decisions less effectively due to allocating the cognitive resource to the particular decision (TR_{RE}) increases as more of the cognitive resource is allocated to that particular decision: $\partial TR_{RE}/\partial \pi_{PD} > 0$. The marginal effect of this increases as more of the resource is assigned to the particular decision ($\partial^2 TR_{RE}/\partial \pi_{PD^2} > 0$), although there may be an initial range over which it remains at zero. The determining factor of this is the ratio Π/Ψ_A. As this ratio declines (meaning the cognitive demand of optimising all the expected decisions increases relative to the available cognitive resource), the expected regret of assigning a marginal unit of the cognitive resource to a particular decision increases. If an individual expects the day to be cognitively undemanding (meaning the available cognitive resource is more than sufficient to meet the optimisation needs of the expected decisions) then allocating more resources to a given decision induces relatively little additional expected regret from taking it away from all subsequent decisions. Conversely, if an individual expects the day to be cognitively demanding (meaning the available cognitive resource is scarce relative to the optimisation needs of the expected decisions) then allocating more

resources to a particular decision induces greater additional expected regret from taking it away from other decisions.

These regrets are represented diagrammatically in Figure 6.1. Optimising the particular decision at hand, according to the standard model of rational choice, requires assigning sufficient cognitive resources to it so the TR_{PD} is reduced to zero. This allocation of the cognitive resource is denoted by $\pi_{PD(OPT)}$. However, this is not the efficient allocation when the expected regret from the remaining decisions is taken into account: the efficient allocation of the cognitive resource to a particular decision is given by equating the marginal expected regret of making the particular decision suboptimally ($MR_{PD} = \partial TR_{PD}/\partial \pi_{PD}$) with the marginal regret arising from reducing the cognitive resources available for the remaining decisions ($MR_{RE} = \partial TR_{RE}/\partial \pi_{PD}$), in absolute terms. This efficient allocation is represented in Figure 6.1A by π^*_{PD}.

The area between the MR_{PD} curve and the horizontal axis between a given allocation of the cognitive resource and that required for optimal decision-making ($\pi_{PD(OPT)}$) represents the total regret from making the particular decision with that allocation of the cognitive resource. The area between the MR_{RE} curve and the horizontal axis between a given allocation of the cognitive resource and that at which MR_{RE} becomes positive (denoted by π'_{PD}) represents the total regret arising from the remaining decisions having allocated that amount of the cognitive resource to the particular decision. The sum of these two areas is what the individual minimises when efficiently allocating his cognitive resource. This is *optimal satisficing*.

It is easier for the analysis that follows to invert the MR_{PD} curve, as that makes absolutely clear the point at which the marginal expected regrets have the same absolute value. Instead of using $MR_{PD} = \beta\pi - \alpha$ as in Figure 6.1B, then, $MR_{PD}^{-1} = \alpha - \beta\pi$ will be used in the diagrams that follow.

(A1.9)   It is assumed that the marginal expected regret curves are linear. In reality this need not be the case. For example, the MR_{PD}^{-1} curve could be horizontal initially (representing a range of cognitive resource allocation over which making the decision suboptimally generates the same expected regret as not making it at all) and thereafter downward sloping.

As Figure 6.1 shows, whether or not the individual decides to allocate sufficient cognitive resources to the particular decision in order to optimise it depends on the relation of the efficient allocation of resources (π^*_{PD}) to that needed for optimisation ($\pi_{PD(OPT)}$). If $\pi^*_{PD} < \pi_{PD(OPT)}$, the individual employs satisficing, whereas if $\pi^*_{PD} \geq \pi_{PD(OPT)}$, the individual optimises. If $\pi^*_{PD} > \pi_{PD(OPT)}$, the individual only allocates $\pi_{PD(OPT)}$ to the decision as further allocation is wasteful (from (A1.2)). To be precise, given the linear nature of the marginal expected regret curves in Figure 6.1, the precise decision rule for the individual is given as equation (6.2), where β and α are the slope and vertical intercept of the MR_{PD}^{-1} curve respectively, and θ and μ are the counterparts for the MR_{PD} curve.

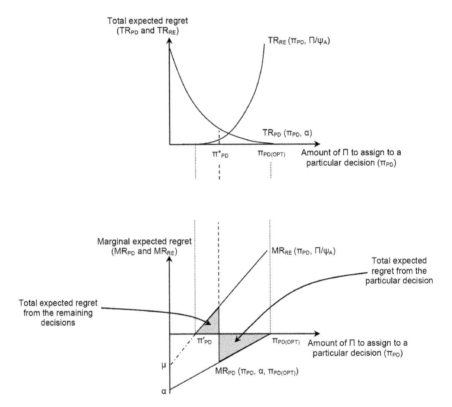

Figure 6.1 Optimal satisficing

$$\pi^{*}_{PD} = \frac{\alpha - \mu}{\beta + \theta} \pi_{PD(OPT)} \text{ then optimise}$$

$$\pi^{*}_{PD} = \frac{\alpha - \mu}{\beta + \theta} \pi_{PD(OPT)} \text{ then satisfice} \qquad (6.2)$$

This analysis leads to the notion of *cognitive surplus*, which is defined as the net expected regret averted from allocating cognitive resources to a particular decision. In effect, cognitive surplus is a measure of the utility the individual receives from actually making a decision, which is known as procedural, as opposed to substantive, utility in the decision-making literature (see Skořepa, 2011). Consider Figure 6.2, which reproduces Figure 6.1 but for a particular decision for which it is just efficient to make it optimally given the limited cognitive resources. The shaded area represents cognitive surplus.

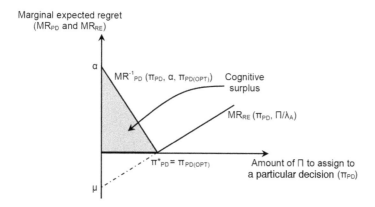

Figure 6.2 Cognitive surplus

Using this model it is possible to analyse the effects of changes to the different variables involved in the cognitive allocation, or higher-order, decision. First, consider a decision that becomes easier to optimise (a reduction in $\pi_{PD(OPT)}$) for some reason, but for which all the other variables remain unchanged. As shown in Figure 6.3, the total expected regret from the particular decision curve pivots inwards from TR_{PD1} to TR_{PD2}, which causes the associated marginal expected regret curve to pivot from MR_{PD1}^{-1} to MR_{PD2}^{-1} in the lower panel. The top panel shows that fewer cognitive resources are now assigned to the decision, but this allocation means the decision is made closer to the result of optimisation than before $\pi_{PD(OPT)1} - \pi^*_{PD1} > \pi_{PD(OPT)2} - \pi^*_{PD2}$. The lower panel shows that the total expected regret from making this particular decision falls as it becomes easier to optimise: the total regret falls from that given by the light and dark shaded triangles of the lower panel to that of only the dark triangle.

Second, consider a decision that becomes increasingly important to make for some reason, but for which all the other variables remain unchanged: only causing the value of α to increase. Figure 6.4 shows the effect of this: the value of α increases from α_1 to α_2; the total and marginal expected regret curves for the particular decision both pivot outwards, from TR_{PD1} to TR_{PD2} and MR_{PD1}^{-1} to MR_{PD2}^{-1}, respectively; and the optimal allocation of the cognitive resource to the decision increases, meaning the decision made is again closer to the result of optimisation. However, the total expected regret from making this decision is also increased, from the light triangle to both the light and dark areas.

The effects caused by changes to the ratio Π/Ψ_A and by combinations of changes can be analysed in similar fashion. This analysis leads to the following three propositions, the proofs of which are presented in Appendix 6.1:

Proposition 1:   The more important the decision, and so the greater the need to make the decision at all (and the larger is α), *ceteris paribus*, the more cognitive resources are assigned to it and so the closer the

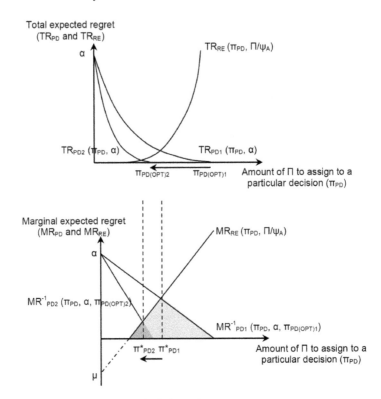

Figure 6.3 Future relevation of helpful information

Proposition 2:
Proposition 3:

decision made will be to the result of optimisation if the decision is being made by satisficing. If the decision is already being optimised, an increase in its importance will have no effect.

Proposition 2:   The greater the cognitive resources needed to make the decision through optimisation (and so the lower is β because $\beta = \alpha/\pi_{PD(OPT)}$), the more resources are allocated to the particular decision.

Proposition 3:   The lower the Π/Ψ_A ratio (and so the larger is θ), the fewer cognitive resources are allocated to the particular decision, meaning the further the decision is from the result of optimisation.

It should be noted that a decision is only made optimally if the amount of cognitive resources required to do so is less than or equal to the amount of resources at which the MR_{RE} becomes positive: the allocation denoted by π'_{PD} in Figure 6.1A. It does not matter how important the decision is, it will not be made optimally (and so will be made through satisficing) if it involves a positive MR_{RE}. In other words, a decision will only be made optimally if it induces no opportunity cost.

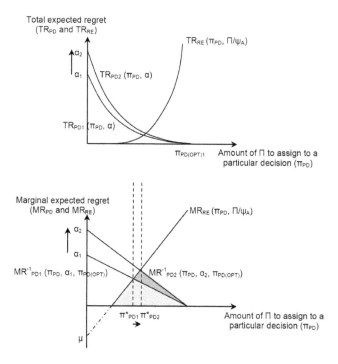

Figure 6.4 Increased importance of the decision

The temporal choice

The analysis so far has examined how an individual allocates his limited cognitive resource across the decisions he expects to make in a period of time; or, alternatively, whether a decision should be made by optimisation or satisficing. It is now necessary to introduce the individual's second problem: whether to make the decision immediately or to postpone it until a specified point in the future.

Each of the main variables in the stage choice is likely to be time dependent. The importance of making the particular decision at all (α) is likely to change over time: delaying the decision may make it increasingly important, for instance, which is the cost of procrastination. Likewise, the amount of cognitive resources required to make the particular decision optimally ($\pi_{PD(OPT)}$) may also change over time: it may become easier to make the decision optimally (and so requires less of the cognitive resource to do so) because new helpful information might be revealed or learning take place. The MR_{RE} might differ from day to day because of the different cognitive demands on the different days relative to the available cognitive resource (different Π/Ψ_A ratios on different days), meaning the slope of the MR_{RE} curve is time dependent. These potential time effects mean it might be efficient, in terms of reducing the level of total expected regret from the decision, to postpone a particular decision until some point in the future rather than making it when it initially arises. Extending the assumption of ecological rationality (A1.6), then, leads to:

(A1.10) The individual is able to calculate the efficient allocation of the cognitive resource to a particular decision, and the resulting total expected regret arising from making that decision, at every future point in time.

From the analysis above, the individual's inter-temporal behavioural rule is given by equation (6.3) below: to allocate the efficient amount of the cognitive resource at the precise time ($\pi^*_{PD,t}$) that minimises the total expected regret from that decision. The total expected regret is given by the sum of the areas beneath the $MR^{-1}_{PD,t}$ curve between the efficient allocation and that required for optimisation, and beneath the $MR_{RE,t}$ curve between the allocation at which MR_{RE} becomes positive and the efficient allocation of cognitive resources.

$$\pi^*_{PD,t} = \operatorname*{argmin}_{\pi^*_{PD,t}} \int_{\pi^*_{PD,t}}^{\pi_{PD(OPT),t}} MR^{-1}_{PD,t}\left(\alpha_t, \pi_{PD}, \pi_{PD(OPT),t}\right)$$

$$+ \int_{\pi'_{PD,t}}^{\pi^*_{PD,t}} MR_{RE,t}\left(\mu, \pi_{PD}, \Pi/\Psi_{A,t}\right) \tag{6.3}$$

Looking at the example analysis above, along with equation (6.3), leads to the following additional propositions:

Proposition 4:   As the importance of making the decision (α) increases over time, *ceteris paribus*, (i) the future cognitive resources to be allocated to the decision by postponing it also increases and (ii) the total expected regret from doing so also increases. The individual makes such decisions immediately as they arise.

Proposition 5:   As the amount of the cognitive resource required to make the particular decision optimally ($\pi_{PD(OPT)}$) falls over time, *ceteris paribus*, the value of β rises, meaning (i) less of the resource is assigned to the particular decision and (ii) the total regret from making the decision efficiently falls over time. The individual procrastinates with such decisions.

Proposition 6:   If the ratio of Π/Ψ_A is lower in the future (meaning future days are expected to be more cognitively demanding), *ceteris paribus*, the value of θ is higher and so in the future (i) less resources are assigned to the particular decision and so (ii) postponing the decision means it is made further from the result of optimisation and so induces greater total expected regret. The individual makes such decisions as they arise rather than postponing them until later.

A model of lower-order decision-making: Hicks and Allen revisited

This section presents an example of a model of lower-order decision-making that builds on the higher-order model presented above.

The decision situation

Before proceeding to the actual lower-order decision-making model, the nature of the considered decision situation should be made explicitly clear. Consumers make series of consumption decisions stretching through their lifetimes. This time horizon can be partitioned in a host of ways: according to budgeting periods, days or phases of life, for example. The analysis of inter-temporal consumption decision-making across these partitions is the focus of the Marshallian consumer (see Clower, 1984; Leijonhufvod, 1974), whereas the focus of the model presented here is on a single decision, about the choice of products, within a given partition. The analysis commences, then, with a consumer who has assigned two budgets to the specific consumption decision with which he is faced: a financial budget (the maximum amount of money that he is willing to spend) and a cognitive budget (the maximum amount of his cognitive resource that he is willing to expend making this decision). The latter budget is directly derived from the higher-order analysis above.

For tractability purposes, and to facilitate the application of a geometric approach, the initial analysis follows the standard convention employed by Hicks and Allen (1934), assuming the availability of only two products: x and y.

The consumption set

A number of simple assumptions are made about the consumer's behaviour in order to motivate the analysis:

(A2.1) Knowledge of purchasing power. The consumer knows the value of his budget (M) and the prices of the available products (P_x and P_y).

(A2.2) Monotonicity. For products that are not 'economic bads', the consumer aspires to consume more rather than less of both.

(A2.3) Knowledge of the available products. The consumer knows the products available in the market, and the available quantity ranges of each, $X = \{x \mid 0 \leq x < \infty\} \subset R_+^N$ and $Y = \{y \mid 0 \leq y < \infty\} \subset R_+^N$. This model is not one of consumer search. It is one that explores the implications of cognitive constraints and deliberation costs. It should be stressed here that $x \in X$ is not a brand within the larger set; it is a quantity.

(A2.4) The consumer has allocated an amount of his limited cognitive resource to the making of this particular decision (following the model outlined in the previous section). This is denoted by π_{PD} (following the notation of the previous section).

(A2.5) Minimum aspired quantities of consumption. Following Simon (1955) and based on A2.1 through A2.4, the consumer establishes minimum aspired quantities of consumption: the minimum physical volumes of x

and y that characterise a satisfactory bundle. Denoted by A^x_{min} and A^y_{min}, they are referred to as the minimum aspirations of x and y, respectively. They are each functions of the consumer's financial and cognitive budgets (the former represented by BL), the price of the product in question and the minimum aspiration level of the other product. This last determinant is important. When establishing the minimum aspiration of x, the consumer considers the minimum aspiration of y because of possible complementarity and substitutability effects between the products. Of course, minimum aspirations could also be influenced by the consumption of other people (relative consumption) but this potential influence is purposefully overlooked here for simplicity.

(A2.6)   Maximum aspired quantities of consumption. The consumer also establishes upper limits to the product quantities that characterise a satisfactory bundle. These are denoted by A^x_{max} and A^y_{max}, and are referred to as the maximum aspirations of these products. It must be stressed that this assumption does not imply the consumer does not want to purchase more than these quantities. Indeed, due to A2.2 the opposite is true. These maximum aspirations simply show the upper limits to the quantities of the products that are possible given the financial and cognitive constraints at the time the consumer establishes minimum aspirations. Specifically, it is assumed the maximum aspiration of one product is determined by the intersection of the minimum aspiration of the other product and the consumer's budget line.

The analysis that follows is grounded on the notion that the consumer possesses an objective function, as in the Hicks and Allen (1934) framework, but does not necessarily choose to make the consumption decision such that it is optimised. The reasoning behind this is outlined in the model of higher-order decision-making in the previous section: given a limited cognitive resource, the consumer chooses to make the consumption decision efficiently rather than optimally in the sense of the standard model of rational choice.

Minimum and maximum aspirations for products x and y are illustrated in Figure 6.5.

The bundles that the consumer deems satisfactory in this case are those contained in the set bounded below by A^x_{min} and A^y_{min}, and bounded above by A^x_{max} and A^y_{max}. This is referred to as the consumer's satisfactory set: $\Omega^s = \{(x, y) \mid A^x_{min} \leq x \leq A^x_{max}, A^y_{min} \leq y \leq A^y_{max}\} \in R^N_+$. As in the Hicks and Allen (1934) framework, the budget line, BL, represents the set of bundles that compose the maximum affordable combinations of x and y given their prevailing prices: it is the set of consumption bundles for which the budget is exhausted, $BL = \{(x, y) \mid P_x x + P_y y = M\}$. The consumer's consumption set, then, is given by the intersection of the satisfactory set and the budget line: $\hat{\Omega} = BL \cap \Omega^s = \{(x, y) \mid A^x_{min} \leq x \leq A^x_{max}, A^y_{min} \leq y \leq A^y_{max}, P_x x + P_y y = M\} \in R^N_+$. This is illustrated in Figure 6.5 by the emboldened segment of the budget line and represents the array of bundles from amongst which the consumed bundle is chosen.

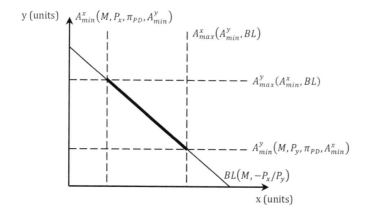

Figure 6.5 Aspired quantities and the budget line

The influence of the cognitive constraint in this decision-making requires examination. As the cognitive resource that the consumer allocates to this decision is increased (and so the greater the value of π_{PD}), the more cognitive effort the consumer is able to invest in making the decision. As such, the greater the cognitive resource allocation, the closer the minimum aspired quantities will be to the amounts of x and y contained within the bundle that maximises the consumer's preference function; the narrower the consumption set; and the closer the choice made will be to that resulting from the standard model of rational choice. Following the notation of the previous section, if the consumer allocates to the decision the amount of his cognitive resource that is sufficient to make the optimal decision ($\pi_{PD(OPT)}$), the consumption set is composed solely of the bundle that optimises his preference function and so maximises his utility. As such, the outcome of the standard model of rational choice is a special case of this model: a requirement that is stressed in the computable economics literature (see, for example, Velupillai, 2000, 2010).

Responding to budget and price changes

(A2.7) Adjustments to minimum aspirations. Based on the notion of decision fatigue, it is assumed the consumer seeks to minimise the number of decisions he makes. As such, the consumer only alters the minimum aspired quantities if either (1) it is no longer possible to purchase a satisfactory bundle or (2) a bundle exists in the market that is now affordable and that satisfies the minimum aspired quantities for both products but is not contained within the consumption set: in other words, it is possible to buy more than the maximum aspired amount of one product and still afford a satisfactory amount of the other.

Consider the two panels in Figure 6.6. The consumer initially establishes minimum and maximum aspirations given by A^x_{min1}, A^y_{min1}, A^x_{max1}, and A^y_{max1}, based on given financial and cognitive budgets and given prices of x and y (with the initial price of x being P_{x1}). Initially, then, the consumer faces a consumption set that incorporates bundles with quantities $x_1 \leq x \leq x_2$, which gives a demand correspondence with the width at P_{x1} shown in Figure 6.6B.

Consider the effect of increasing the price of product x. Each time the price increases, the budget line pivots inwards along the horizontal axis, as in the Hicks and Allen (1934) framework and as shown in Figure 6.6A from BL_1 to BL_2. For a range of such price increases, the consumer is not compelled to alter his minimum aspired quantities because it remains possible to purchase a satisfactory bundle. Over this range, then, the resulting demand correspondence (shown in Figure 6.6B) is characterised by a constant minimum amount of x, as determined by A^x_{min1} (in this case x_1). However, the upper limit to the amount of x contained within the consumption set, and so of the demand correspondence, falls because of the interaction between the pivoting budget line and A^x_{min1}. This causes a narrowing of the demand correspondence for product x. This continues with further increases in the price of x until a price of P_{x2}, at which the consumer cannot afford a satisfactory bundle of goods as defined by A^x_{min1} and A^y_{min1}. At this price the consumption set is empty and the demand correspondence collapses, compelling the consumer to alter his minimum aspired quantities of the two products.

Changes to minimum aspired quantities caused by changes in price (or income) are subject to the same two pressures that operate within the standard framework:

1   *Income effect.* An increase in price causes a reduction in the consumer's real purchasing power. The consumer realises this and so alters A^x_{min} and A^y_{min} accordingly: downwards for a normal good and upwards for an inferior good.

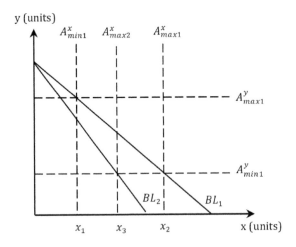

Figure 6.6A Responding to a price change

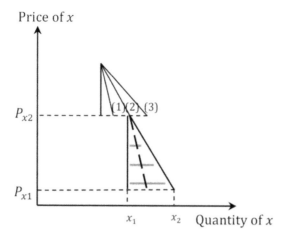

Figure 6.6B Demand correspondence caused by increases in price

2 *Substitution effect.* An increase in the price of x means it is now relatively more expensive than y. This causes a weakly positive substitution in minimum aspired quantities away from x and towards y, depending on the relationship between them.

The demand correspondence for a normal or inferior good resulting from a series of increases in its price is illustrated in Figure 6.6B. The price range from 0 to P_{x2} reflects the range of increases in its price over which the consumer does not alter minimum aspired quantities. Once the price reaches P_{x2}, the consumer is compelled to alter them. Consider first the substitution effect on A^x_{min}. This is negative because the consumer substitutes desired consumption towards the relatively cheaper product. The income effect is less clear. For a normal good it is also negative, but for an inferior good it is positive. The Hicks and Allen (1934) framework suggests that for a normal good the substitution and income effects operate in the same direction, and that for an inferior good the substitution effect outweighs the income effect. In both cases, then, the consumer reduces A^x_{min}, causing the vertical lower bound of the demand correspondence to shift inwards. Consider now the effect on A^y_{min}. The substitution effect on this is positive because the consumer switches desired consumption towards product y. The income effect again depends on whether it is normal or inferior. If it is inferior, the positive income effect strengthens the positive substitution effect, inducing the consumer to increase A^y_{min} and causing the upper bound of the demand correspondence to resemble the line denoted by (1). If it is normal, and the income effect acting upon A^y_{min} either outweighs or cancels out the corresponding substitution effect, meaning A^y_{min} is reduced or unaltered, the upper bound resembles that denoted by (2). If it is normal and the income effect strongly outweighs the substitution effect, A^y_{min} could be sufficiently reduced for the upper bound of the correspondence to resemble that labelled (3).

The same process of analysis could be worked through to generate the possible demand correspondences for a good arising from a sequence of reductions in its price, and also to generate the Engels correspondences arising for different goods from sequences of both income increases and reductions. Instead of outlining such analysis here, the propositions to which this alternative model of choice leads, which distinguish it from the Hicks and Allen (1934) framework, are examined and discussed:

Proposition 1:   Consumer behaviour is characterised by regular kinks as consumers adjust their minimum aspired quantities in response to increasing prices and falling budgets. However, it adjusts smoothly in response to falling prices and expanding budgets: kinks do not appear with such changes.

With the ever-expanding availability of household panel data, such kinks in consumption behaviour are indeed being observed. Puller and Greening (1999), for instance, observe significant differences in the immediate and overall responses to increases in petrol prices, finding that 'consumers initially respond to a price rise with a much larger decrease in consumption than would be indicated by the total elasticity' (page 37). In other words, these authors find a low impact on the demand for petrol of an increase in its price more than one quarter in the past, whereas that of a contemporaneous increase in price is much higher. They explain this observation by suggesting consumers postpone long journeys, such as holidays, until times when petrol is not so expensive. Although this is logical, the results can also be explained with reference to the alternative model presented above. Consumers reduce their petrol consumption due to rising prices until doing so becomes intolerable, at which point they reassess their priorities in consumption and make the necessary adjustments to their bundles such that they contain greater amounts of petrol again. The total elasticity arising from such behaviour is significantly lower than the impact (immediate) elasticity. Precisely this could arise from case (3) in Figure 6.6B.

Proposition 2:   Consumer behaviour exhibits ranges of insensitivity: price ranges across which the price can change without compelling the consumer to alter consumption choices.

Such ranges of insensitivity around predetermined reference points have been clearly identified in the literature. For example, Kalyanaram and Little (1994) and Rao and Sieben (1992) demonstrate that as long as the price of a product remains within certain bounds of a reference level (the price to which consumers' expectations have adapted), consumers will not alter the amounts they consume in response to price changes in the consumption of soft drinks and blazers, respectively. This links to the extensive evidence for the 'status quo bias' (see Ariely,

2009; Kahneman, 2011): consumers appear willing to bear additional expenditure, or to forego the possibility of greater consumption, to maintain the status-quo as long as the foregone utility is not perceived too large.

Proposition 3:   Observed consumer behaviour need not reflect true underlying preferences. For example, the consumer may not alter behaviour if the experienced price change lies entirely within a range of insensitivity, but that is not evidence of underlying preferences that are insensitive to price changes.

This proposition is supported by the work of Ariely *et al.* (2003), which demonstrates that demand curves estimated from market data need not reveal true consumer preferences in any normatively significant sense. They demonstrate from six experiments that consumer valuations of familiar products can easily be perceived as being ordered, but that in fact they cannot be interpreted as emanating from rational responses to information. The authors propose that individual choices are governed by 'coherent arbitrariness': choices are coherently adjusted according to changes in information but around a seemingly arbitrary, predetermined, benchmark. The alternative model presented above can be interpreted in this way: consumers establish minimum aspired levels of consumption, which they then coherently adjust in response to changes in their real purchasing power.

Conclusions

The purpose of the methodological approach that has been presented in this chapter is to address the fundamental criticism of the behavioural economics and bounded rationality literatures: that they are yet to propose a viable general alternative model of decision-making to rival the standard model of rational choice, instead consisting of a variety of specifically applied models based on rather arbitrary and *ad hoc* assumptions. The approach is based on viewing decision-making as a two-step process. In the first step, a decision-maker decides how much of his limited cognitive resource to allocate to a particular question or sequence of questions. Weakly supported by anecdotal evidence, and in the absence of evidence to the contrary, it is assumed that this higher-order decision is made according to the standard model of rational choice and that the decision-maker allocates the efficient amount of his cognitive resource to each decision, based on his expectations regarding the number and importance of the other decisions (and other acts of volition) that he will be required to make before being able to replenish his cognitive reserve. This then determines the degree to which the decision-maker's actual choice in a particular decision is optimal in the standard sense: the lower-order decision. In other words, it determines the degree to which the lower-order decision is made in a satisficing manner.

A simple model of such decision-making has been sketched in this chapter, which uses the consumption decision situation examined by Hicks and Allen (1934) as the example for the lower-order decision. It has been shown that, grounded on relatively undemanding behavioural assumptions and developing the framework of Simon (1955), this alternative to the standard theory of value leads to a number of propositions about market behaviour that are supported by empirical and observational findings.

This approach rationalises decision-making at the higher-order level. It also focuses on the *degree* to which decisions depart from the predictions of the standard model of rational choice and the *direction* of such departures, rather than on the *precise options* that will be chosen, and the *precise processes* that will be employed, by a decision-maker in a given situation. This change of focus from that typically adopted in the behavioural economics literature requires empirical and experimental investigation into these degrees and directions in different decision situations: an avenue of research that is yet to be taken within the literature. However, such a research programme within behavioural economics could inform the development of a general, overarching model of decision-making to rival that of the standard model of rational choice, thereby overcoming the fundamental criticism outlined above.

References

Ariely, D. (2009) *Predictably Irrational: The Hidden Forces that Shape Our Decisions*, London: Harper-Collins.

Ariely, D., Loewenstein, G. and Prelec, D. (2003) 'Coherent arbitrariness: stable demand curves without stable preferences', *Quarterly Journal of Economics* 118, 73–105.

Augenblick, N. and Nicholson, S. (2009) 'Choice fatigue: the effect of making previous choices on decision-making', *Berkeley Research Paper*, San Francisco, CA: University of California.

Basov, S. (2006) 'The mechanics of choice', in Tavidze, A. (ed.) *Progress in Economics Research, Vol. 10*, New York: Nova Science Publishers, 55–64.

Baumeister, R.F., Bratslavsky, E., Muraven, M. and Tice, D.M. (1998) 'Ego depletion: is the active self a limited resource?', *Journal of Personality and Social Psychology* 74, 1252–1265.

Baumeister, R.F., Heatherton, T.F. and Tice, D.M. (1994) *Losing Control: How and Why People Fail at Self-regulation,* San Diego, CA: Academic Press.

Baumeister, R.F. and Tierney, J. (2011) *Willpower: Rediscovering Our Greatest Strength,* London: Allen Lane, The Penguin Group.

Bernheim, D. and Rangel A. (2009) 'Beyond revealed preference: choice-theoretic foundations for behavioral welfare economics', *Quarterly Journal of Economics* 124, 51–105.

Boatwright, P. and Nunes, J.C. (2001) 'Reducing assortment: an attribute-based approach', *Journal of Marketing* 65, 50–63.

Bucciol, A., Houser, D. and Piovesan, M. (2011) 'Temptation and productivity: a field experiment with children', *Journal of Economic Behavior & Organization* 78, 126–136.

Cadena, B.C. and Keys, B.J. (2013) 'Can self-control explain avoiding free money? Evidence from interest-free student loans', *Review of Economics & Statistics* 95, 1117–1129.

Clower, R.W (1984) *Money and Markets: Essays by Robert W. Clower*, edited by D.A. Walker, Cambridge, UK: Cambridge University Press.

Cosmides, L. and Tooby, J. (1994) 'Better than rational: evolutionary psychology and the invisible hand', *American Economic Review* 84, 327–332.

Dickhaut, J., Smith, V., Xin, B. and Rustichini, A. (2013) 'Human economic choice as costly information processing', *Journal of Economic Behavior & Orgnization* 94, 206–221.

Gilboa, I. and Schmeidler, D. (1995) 'Case-based decision theory', *Quarterly Journal of Economics* 110, 605–639.

Hardie, B.G.S., Johnson, E.J. and Fader, P.S. (1993) 'Modeling loss aversion and reference dependence effects on brand choice', *Marketing Science* 12, 378–394.

Hicks, J.R. and Allen, R.G.D. (1934) 'A reconsideration of the theory of value, part 1', *Economica* 1, 52–76.

Iyengar, S.S. and Kamenica, E. (2010) 'Choice proliferation, simplicity seeking, and asset allocation', *Journal of Public Economics* 94, 530–539.

Iyengar, S.S. and Lepper, M.R. (2000) 'When choice is demotivating: can one desire too much of a good thing?', *Journal of Personality and Social Psychology* 79, 995–1006.

Kahneman, D. (2011) *Thinking, Fast and Slow*, New York: Farrar, Straus and Giroux.

Kalayci, K. and Potters, J. (2011) 'Buyer confusion and market prices', *International Journal of Industrial Organization* 29, 14–22.

Kalyanaram, G. and Little, J.D.C. (1994) 'An empirical analysis of latitude of price acceptance in consumer package goods', *Journal of Consumer Research* 21, 408–418.

Leijonhufvod, A. (1974) 'Maximisation and Marshall: the Marshall Lectures', Mimeo, University of Cambridge and UCLA.

Levav, J., Heitmann, M., Herrmann, A. and Iyengar, S.S. (2010) 'Order in product customization decisions: evidence from field experiments', *Journal of Political Economy* 118, 274–300.

Mackowiak, B. and Wiederholt, M. (2012) 'Information processing and limited liability', *American Economic Review Papers and Proceedings* 102, 30–34.

Marshall, A. (1920) *Principles of Economics*, Volume 1, Eighth Edition, London: Macmillan.

Miravete, E.J. and Palacios-Huerta, I. (2014) 'Consumer inertia, choice dependence, and learning from experience in a repeated decision problem', *Review of Economics and Statistics* 96, 524–537.

Muraven, M., Tice, D.M. and Baumeister, R.F. (1998) 'Self-control as limited resource: regulatory depletion patterns', *Journal of Personality and Social Psychology* 74, 774–789.

Puller, S.L. and Greening, L.A. (1999) 'Household adjustment to gasoline price change: an analysis using 9 years of US survey data', *Energy Economics* 21, 37–52.

Putler, D. (1992) 'Incorporating reference price effects into a theory of consumer choice', *Marketing Science* 11, 287–309.

Rao, A.R. and Sieben, W.A. (1992) 'The effect of prior knowledge on price acceptability and the type of information examined', *Journal of Consumer Research* 19, 256–270.

Simon, H.A. (1955) 'A behavioural model of rational choice', *Quarterly Journal of Economics* 69, 99–118.

Skořepa, M. (2011) *Decision-making: A Behavioural Economic Approach*, Basingstoke, UK: Palgrave Macmillan.

Spiegler, R. (2011). *Bounded Rationality and Industrial Organization*, Oxford: Oxford University Press.

Stigler, G.J. and Becker, G.S. (1977) 'De gustibus non est disputendum', *American Economic Review* 67, 76–90.

Tirole, J. (2009) 'Cognition and incomplete contracts', *American Economic Review* 99, 265–294.

Velupillai, K.V. (2000) *Computable Economics: The Arne Ryde Memorial Lectures*, Oxford, UK: Oxford University Press.

Velupillai, K.V. (2010) *Computable Foundations for Economics: Methodology and Philosophy*, Abingdon, UK: Routledge.

7   Concluding thoughts

The intention in writing this monograph was to address four issues, which are outlined in the introductory chapter. In this final chapter, the findings relating to each of these issues are first summarised, before moving onto a brief overview of the key avenue of future research that has been proposed.

Summaries

(1) The nature of the different evolutionary paths of the literatures of behavioural economics and bounded rationality

The bounded rationality and behavioural economics literatures are both concerned with decision-making at the lower-order level of choice. However, their specific focuses are different. Works of bounded rationality tend to focus on the wider economic consequences of decision-making in situations in which the decision-maker is unable to act as if according to the standard model of rational choice because of a discrepancy between his cognitive capacity and the complexity of the decisions he faces. These works largely analyse abstract, theoretical models of decision-making that are motivated by observations of actual behaviour. Works of behavioural economics, by contrast, tend to focus on the precise cognitive processes and influences involved in decision-making, including the nature of people's preferences and the way in which their decision-making can be manipulated. To do this, they primarily conduct experiments, of a range of different types, drawing inferences about behaviour from observations of how subjects respond to predetermined information or to the actions of others.

A greater proportion of the works of bounded rationality are published in the highest ranking academic journals in economics; whereas the greatest proportion of those of behavioural economics are published in economics journals that are generally considered to be in the second tier. This is perhaps unsurprising given the more general and theoretical nature of bounded rationality and the more situation-specific nature of behavioural economics: the journals that constitute the highest rank in economics are largely generalist and of a theoretical leaning, whereas those in the second rank tend to be the top, specific field journals. However, in terms of the academic impact of the two literatures, which is measured by the number of citations that they each receive within the wider literature, there is no significant difference between them when relevant factors have been controlled.

(2) The consequences of this evolutionary divide

The two literatures are completely compatible, with behavioural economics opening up the black box of people's preferences and cognitive processes, which can then be integrated into the theoretical works of bounded rationality. However, the degree to which the powers of the two literatures are harnessed is limited, with each largely continuing to pursue its own evolutionary path. In terms of Figure 5.6, it could be argued that each of the literatures is moving further away from the point of optimal analytical power, rather than moving the discipline as a whole towards the objective of an optimal modelling approach. As such, the literatures are fully compatible but that compatibility is not being fully utilised.

(3) The advantages and disadvantages for economics as a whole of these two fields evolving in the different directions they have taken

The beneficial impact of the establishment and growth of the separate field of behavioural economics should not be underestimated. Focusing explicitly on the processes involved in economic decision-making has opened up a vast array of new avenues of research that economists can pursue and has deepened our understanding of both the microeconomic functioning of individual markets and the macroeconomic functioning of the economy as a whole. It has also drawn an uncountable number of students into the economics fold, who otherwise would not have been attracted by the traditional abstract and mathematical approach of the subject. It has also increased the relevance of the subject, which has been particularly timely given the discontentment that arose in the aftermath of the financial crash of 2008. These benefits would not have been realised had the discipline relied solely on the bounded rationality paradigm for advancements in this area.

However, taking these distinct evolutionary paths has lead to a number of criticisms of these fields within the literature. Primary among these is that the literatures of bounded rationality and behavioural economics have succeeded in generating a vast array of understanding about specific decision-making in particular situations, but that they are yet to present a single, unifying framework through which economic decision-making as a whole can be understood: they have not yet provided a satisfactory answer to the question of which specific behaviour can be assumed to occur in a new, given decision situation. The problem is that this leaves economic analysis that is motivated by behavioural assumptions open to the accusation of being based on rather arbitrary and *ad hoc* foundations.

(4) The lessons that can be taken from an assessment of all of the above

The fruitfulness of bounded rationality and behavioural economics has been astonishing (regarding so many different criteria), and it is perhaps not surprising that they are yet to present a satisfactory alternative to the standard model of rational choice, which has been developed over the course of the last century. However, for their full analytical potential to be realised there is a need for such an alternative framework. The central proposition to be drawn from this monograph is that this framework lies in the mutually reinforcing collaboration of these fields.

Towards an overarching model of behavioural economic decision-making

The corollary to the central proposition above is that focusing on the *degree* to which economic decisions depart from the predictions of the standard model of rational choice and on the *direction* of such departures is a potentially fertile avenue of research as economists seek to develop an overarching model of behavioural economic decision-making. This is in contrast to the approach generally adopted in the literature, which examines the *precise cognitive processes* that are employed by decision-makers and the *precise decisions* to which they lead.

This proposed approach involves viewing decision-making as a two-stage process. In the first (higher-order) stage, the decision-maker allocates his limited cognitive resources across the (expected) decisions he faces in the period until he is able to replenish his cognitive reserve. This cognitive allocation then determines the degree to which the decision-maker can then make each particular decision as if according to the standard model of rational choice. It provides a framework in which every type of decision can be analysed, and in which the strengths of the bounded rationality and behavioural economics literatures can be harnessed together. However, it requires there to be a new focus within behavioural economics. As Miravete and Palacios-Huerta (2014, pages 524–525) comment:

> We would expect that various decades of research would have produced systematic empirical evidence on the type of decision problems where consumers behave irrationally and the types of problems where they are rational, on how consumer behavior depends on the cost of acquiring and processing information relative to the benefits of better decision making, and on the types of situations where subjects tend to reason accurately or tend to make permanent errors. The fact is, however, that we are far from this ideal.

It is precisely this systematic empirical evidence that is required for the proposed approach to be implemented. As such, there is need for the bounded rationality and behavioural economics literatures to engage in the iterative procedure illustrated in Figure 7.1. This involves behavioural economics informing the construction of bounded rationality models with evidence regarding the degrees and directions of departures from the standard model of rational choice in different decision situations, and with developments in bounded rationality informing the objectives of studies in behavioural economics. Only through such a repeated iterative process can these fields fully address the fundamental criticism to which they are exposed.

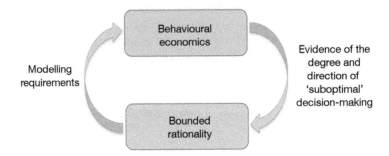

Figure 7.1 The required collaboration between behavioural economics and bounded
rationality

Scientific progress entails the ever-deepening understanding of natural
phenomena, with the focus of study being continually shifted to the unknown
forces that lie behind the processes we observe. Economics has now reached the
stage at which the analysis of microeconomic decision-making should be pushed
to the deeper (alternatively raised to the higher) level at which decision-makers
decide *how* they make their choices. It is only by doing this that we will be able to
discern a unifying framework through which behaviour can be understood and
modelled. Both bounded rationality and behavioural economics have significant
functions to perform in this: functions that are interrelated, requiring their efforts
to be drawn together.

Reference

Miravete, E.J. and Palacios-Huerta, I. (2014) 'Consumer inertia, choice dependence, and
learning from experience in a repeated decision problem', *Review of Economics &
Statistics* 96, 524–537.

Appendix 2.1 Behavioral economics

Primary articles

Authors	Date	Article title	Journal	Rank	Citations
Fudenberg & Levine	Jan 2012	Timing And Self-Control	*Econometrica*	4	5
Heydenreich *et al.*	Jan 2009	Characterization Of Revenue Equivalence	*Econometrica*	4	5
Siegel	Jan 2009	All-Pay Contests	*Econometrica*	4	22
Govindan & Wilson	Jan 2009	On Forward Induction	*Econometrica*	4	2
Teague	Nov 2008	Problems With Coordination In Two-Player Games: Comment On 'Computational Complexity And Communication.'	*Econometrica*	4	5
De Clippel & Serrano	Nov 2008	Marginal Contributions And Externalities In The Value	*Econometrica*	4	8
Weintraub *et al.*	Nov 2008	Markov Perfect Industry Dynamics With Many Firms	*Econometrica*	4	18
Blundell *et al.*	Nov 2008	Best Nonparametric Bounds On Demand Responses	*Econometrica*	4	14
Conlon	Jan 2009	Two New Conditions Supporting The First-Order Approach To Multisignal Principal-Agent Problems	*Econometrica*	4	6
Fortnow & Vohra	Jan 2009	The Complexity Of Forecast Testing	*Econometrica*	4	4
Horner & Vieille	Jan 2009	Public Vs. Private Offers In The Market For Lemons	*Econometrica*	4	0
Vanberg	Nov 2008	Why Do People Keep Their Promises? An Experimental Test Of Two Explanations	*Econometrica*	4	34
Charles *et al.*	May 2009	Conspicuous Consumption And Race	*Quarterly Journal of Economics*	4	36
Cesarini *et al.*	May 2009	Genetic Variation In Preferences For Giving And Risk Taking	*Quarterly Journal of Economics*	4	15
Brown *et al.*	Feb 2009	Learning And Visceral Temptation In Dynamic Saving Experiments	*Quarterly Journal of Economics*	4	10
Bernheim & Rangel	Feb 2009	Beyond Revealed Preference: Choice-Theoretic Foundations For Behavioral Welfare Economics	*Quarterly Journal of Economics*	4	22

Authors	Date	Article title	Journal	Rank	Citations
De Clippel	Oct 2014	Behavioral Implementation	American Economic Review	4	0
Shiller	June 2014	Speculative Asset Prices	American Economic Review	4	0
Kaplow	May 2011	Optimal Proof Burdens, Deterrence, And The Chilling Of Desirable Behavior	American Economic Review	4	0
Salant	Apr 2011	Procedural Analysis Of Choice Rules With Applications To Bounded Rationality	American Economic Review	4	3
Rabin	May 2013	An Approach To Incorporating Psychology Into Economics	American Economic Review	4	1
Barberis	May 2013	The Psychology Of Tail Events: Progress And Challenges	American Economic Review	4	0
Esponda	Sept 2008	Behavioral Equilibrium In Economies With Adverse Selection	American Economic Review	4	7
Gul & Pesendorfer	May 2007	Welfare Without Happiness	American Economic Review	4	2
Blattman & Miguel	Mar 2010	Civil War	Journal of Economic Literature	4	73
Crawford	June 2013	Boundedly Rational Versus Optimization-Based Models Of Strategic Thinking And Learning In Games	Journal of Economic Literature	4	1
Dellavigna	June 2009	Psychology And Economics: Evidence From The Field	Journal of Economic Literature	4	112
Kumbhakar et al.	Jan 2013	A Zero Inefficiency Stochastic Frontier Model	Journal of Econometrics	4	0
Eberly et al.	May 2012	What Explains The Lagged-Investment Effect?	Journal of Monetary Economics	4	4
Evren	Nov 2012	Altruism And Voting: A Large-Turnout Result That Does Not Rely On Civic Duty Or Cooperative Behavior	Journal of Economic Theory	4	0
Krishna & Morgan	Nov 2012	Voluntary Voting: Costs And Benefits	Journal of Economic Theory	4	2

Authors	Date	Article title	Journal	Rank	Citations
Bommier *et al.*	July 2012	Comparative Risk Aversion: A Formal Approach With Applications To Saving Behavior	*Journal of Economic Theory*	4	1
Stahl	Oct 2014	Heterogeneity Of Preferences	*Review of Economics and Statistics*	4	0
Cadena & Keys	Oct 2013	Can Self-Control Explain Avoiding Free Money? Evidence From Interest-Free Student Loans	*Review of Economics and Statistics*	4	0
Miravete & Palacios-Huerta	July 2014	Consumer Inertia, Choice Dependence, And Learning From Experience In A Repeated Decision Problem	*Review of Economics and Statistics*	4	1
Takanori & Goto	Nov 2009	Simultaneous Measurement Of Time And Risk Preferences: Stated Preference Discrete Choice Modeling Analysis Depending On Smoking Behavior	*International Economic Review*	4	5
Astebro *et al.*	June 2014	Seeking The Roots Of Entrepreneurship: Insights From Behavioral Economics	*Journal of Economic Perspectives*	4	0
Barberis	Dec 2013	Thirty Years Of Prospect Theory In Economics: A Review And Assessment	*Journal of Economic Perspectives*	4	5
Benartzi *et al.*	Sept 2011	Annuitization Puzzles	*Journal of Economic Perspectives*	4	12
Oreopoulos & Salvanes	Dec 2011	Priceless: The Nonpecuniary Benefits Of Schooling	*Journal of Economic Perspectives*	4	15
Frey *et al.*	Dec 2011	Behavior Under Extreme Conditions: The Titanic Disaster	*Journal of Economic Perspectives*	4	1
Abramitzky	Dec 2011	Lessons From The Kibbutz On The Equality—Incentives Trade-Off	*Journal of Economic Perspectives*	4	3
Itzhak *et al.*	June 2008	Probability And Uncertainty In Economic Modeling	*Journal of Economic Perspectives*	4	5

Authors	Date	Article title	Journal	Rank	Citations
Ashraf et al.	June 2005	Adam Smith, Behavioral Economist	Journal of Economic Perspectives	4	23
Bengtsson & Engstrom	June 2014	Replacing Trust With Control: A Field Test Of Motivation Crowd Out Theory	The Economic Journal	4	0
Bhaskar	Jan 2009	Rational Adversaries? Evidence From Randomised Trials In One Day Cricket	The Economic Journal	4	1
Rubinstein	Oct 2007	Instinctive And Cognitive Reasoning: A Study Of Response Times	The Economic Journal	4	26
Chen et al.	Nov 2012	Threshold Management In A Coupled Economic–Ecological System	Journal of Environmental Economics and Management	4	0
Kallbekken et al.	July 2011	Do You Not Like Pigou, Or Do You Not Understand Him? Tax Aversion And Revenue Recycling In The Lab	Journal of Environmental Economics and Management	4	3
Heyes & Kapur	Nov 2012	Community Pressure For Green Behavior	Journal of Environmental Economics and Management	4	0
Samuelson	Dec 2008	Asymmetric Or Symmetric Time Preference And Discounting In Many Facets Of Economic Theory: A Miscellany	Journal of Risk and Uncertainty	4	2
Bettin et al.	Nov 2012	Endogeneity And Sample Selection In A Model For Remittances	Journal of Development Economics	3	3
Thornton	Nov 2012	HIV Testing, Subjective Beliefs And Economic Behavior	Journal of Development Economics	3	2
Cason et al.	Feb 2012	Behavioral Spillovers In Coordination Games	European Economic Review	3	3
List & Samek	Jan 2015	The Behavioralist As Nutritionist: Leveraging Behavioral Economics To Improve Child Food Choice And Consumption	Journal of Health Economics	3	0
Sloan et al.	May 2014	The Behavioral Economics Of Drunk Driving	Journal of Health Economics	3	0

Authors	Date	Article title	Journal	Rank	Citations
Bradford & Dolan	Dec 2010	Getting Used To It: The Adaptive Global Utility Model	Journal of Health Economics	3	2
Silverman et al.	May 2014	Distinguishing The Role Of Authority "In" And Authority "To"	Journal of Public Economics	3	0
McCluskey et al.	Feb 2012	From Default To Choice: Adding Healthy Options To Kids' Menus	American Journal of Agricultural Economics	3	0
Gundersen et al.	Feb 2012	Insights Into Obesity From A Behavioral Economics Perspective: Discussion	American Journal of Agricultural Economics	3	0
Arunachalam et al.	Aug 2009	An Empirical Investigation Into The Excessive-Choice Effect	American Journal of Agricultural Economics	3	2
Ghosh & Blackhurst	Sept 2014	Energy Savings And The Rebound Effect With Multiple Energy Services And Efficiency Correlation	Ecological Economics	3	0
Kits et al.	Sept 2014	Do Conservation Auctions Crowd Out Voluntary Environmentally Friendly Activities?	Ecological Economics	3	0
Rona-Tas & Guseva	May 2013	Information And Consumer Credit In Central And Eastern Europe	Journal of Comparative Economics	3	2
Dohmen	Oct 2014	Behavioral Labor Economics: Advances And Future Directions	Labour Economics	3	0
Das & Stratman	Jan 2013	Options And Structured Products In Behavioral Portfolios	Journal of Economic Dynamics & Control	3	1
Frijns et al.	Nov 2010	Behavioral Heterogeneity In The Option Market	Journal of Economic Dynamics & Control	3	6
Karmi	Jan 2009	A Reformulation Of The Maxmin Expected Utility Model With Application To Agency Theory	Journal of Mathematical Economics	3	2
Manea	Sept 2008	Unique Induced Preference Representations	Journal of Mathematical Economics	3	0

Authors	Date	Article title	Journal	Rank	Citations
Roth & Voskort	Nov 2014	Stereotypes And False Consensus: How Financial Professionals Predict Risk Preferences	*Journal of Economic Behavior & Organization*	3	0
Gherzi et al.	Nov 2014	The Meerkat Effect: Personality And Market Returns Affect Investors' Portfolio Monitoring Behaviour	*Journal of Economic Behavior & Organization*	3	0
Kliger et al.	Nov 2014	Empirical Behavioral Finance	*Journal of Economic Behavior & Organization*	3	0
Harding & Hsiaw	Nov 2014	Goal Setting And Energy Conservation	*Journal of Economic Behavior & Organization*	3	0
Mandler	Jan 2014	Indecisiveness In Behavioral Welfare Economics	*Journal of Economic Behavior & Organization*	3	0
Bolton & Ockenfels	Jan 2014	Does Laboratory Trading Mirror Behavior In Real World Markets? Fair Bargaining And Competitive Bidding On Ebay	*Journal of Economic Behavior & Organization*	3	0
Ockenfels & Werner	Jan 2014	Scale Manipulation In Dictator Games	*Journal of Economic Behavior & Organization*	3	0
Banerjee & Shogren	Jan 2014	Bidding Behavior Given Point And Interval Values In A Second-Price Auction	*Journal of Economic Behavior & Organization*	3	0
Neanidis & Papadopoulou	July 2013	Crime, Fertility, And Economic Growth: Theory And Evidence	*Journal of Economic Behavior & Organization*	3	0
Barham et al.	Jan 2014	The Roles Of Risk And Ambiguity In Technology Adoption	*Journal of Economic Behavior & Organization*	3	0
Koenig & Wagener	June 2013	Tax Structure And Government Expenditures With Tax Equity Concerns	*Journal of Economic Behavior & Organization*	3	0
Tonin & Vlassopoulos	June 2013	Experimental Evidence Of Self-Image Concerns As Motivation For Giving	*Journal of Economic Behavior & Organization*	3	0

Authors	Date	Article title	Journal	Rank	Citations
Sheremeta & Shields	Oct 2013	Do Liars Believe? Beliefs And Other-Regarding Preferences In Sender–Receiver Games	*Journal of Economic Behavior & Organization*	3	2
Rietz et al.	Oct 2013	Transparency, Efficiency And The Distribution Of Economic Welfare In Pass-Through Investment Trust Games	*Journal of Economic Behavior & Organization*	3	0
Dickhaut et al.	Oct 2013	Human Economic Choice As Costly Information Processing	*Journal of Economic Behavior & Organization*	3	0
Dickhaut et al.	Oct 2013	High Stakes Behavior With Low Payoffs: Inducing Preferences With Holt–Laury Gambles	*Journal of Economic Behavior & Organization*	3	0
Bigoni et al.	Oct 2013	Strategies Of Cooperation And Punishment Among Students And Clerical Workers	*Journal of Economic Behavior & Organization*	3	0
Harrison et al.	Oct 2013	Inducing Risk Neutral Preferences With Binary Lotteries: A Reconsideration	*Journal of Economic Behavior & Organization*	3	2
Stahl	Oct 2013	An Experimental Test Of The Efficacy Of A Simple Reputation Mechanism To Solve Social Dilemmas	*Journal of Economic Behavior & Organization*	3	0
Kriss et al.	Sept 2013	Implicit Vs. Explicit Deception In Ultimatum Games With Incomplete Information	*Journal of Economic Behavior & Organization*	3	3
Hoffman et al.	Sept 2013	The Royal Lie	*Journal of Economic Behavior & Organization*	3	0
Sandroni & Squintani	Sept 2013	Overconfidence And Asymmetric Information: The Case Of Insurance	*Journal of Economic Behavior & Organization*	3	1
Lightle	Sept 2013	Harmful Lie Aversion And Lie Discovery In Noisy Expert Advice Games	*Journal of Economic Behavior & Organization*	3	1
Pirinsky	July 2013	Confidence And Economic Attitudes	*Journal of Economic Behavior & Organization*	3	1

Authors	Date	Article title	Journal	Rank	Citations
Bernard et al.	July 2013	The Subgroup Problem: When Can Binding Voting On Extractions From A Common Pool Resource Overcome The Tragedy Of The Commons?	Journal of Economic Behavior & Organization	3	0
Charness et al.	July 2013	Experimental Methods: Extra-Laboratory Experiments-Extending The Reach Of Experimental Economics	Journal of Economic Behavior & Organization	3	0
Andreozzi	June 2013	Learning To Be Fair	Journal of Economic Behavior & Organization	3	0
Cornelissen et al.	June 2013	Fairness Spillovers—The Case Of Taxation	Journal of Economic Behavior & Organization	3	0
Chandler & Kapelner	June 2013	Breaking Monotony With Meaning: Motivation In Crowdsourcing Markets	Journal of Economic Behavior & Organization	3	2
McAlvanah & Moul	June 2013	The House Doesn't Always Win: Evidence Of Anchoring Among Australian Bookies	Journal of Economic Behavior & Organization	3	1
Slonim et al.	June 2013	Opting-In: Participation Bias In Economic Experiments	Journal of Economic Behavior & Organization	3	1
Elsinger	July 2013	Comment On: A New Test For Chaos And Determinism Based On Symbolic Dynamics	Journal of Economic Behavior & Organization	3	0
Bjornskov et al.	July 2013	Inequality And Happiness: When Perceived Social Mobility And Economic Reality Do Not Match	Journal of Economic Behavior & Organization	3	2
Thomas & Wang	July 2013	Optimal Punishment In Contests With Endogenous Entry	Journal of Economic Behavior & Organization	3	0
Dower & Pfutze	July 2013	Specificity Of Control: The Case Of Mexico's Ejido Reform	Journal of Economic Behavior & Organization	3	0

Authors	Date	Article title	Journal	Rank	Citations
Van Hoorn & Maseland	July 2013	Does A Protestant Work Ethic Exist? Evidence From The Well-Being Effect Of Unemployment	*Journal of Economic Behavior & Organization*	3	0
Chen et al.	June 2013	Too Smart To Be Selfish? Measures Of Cognitive Ability, Social Preferences, And Consistency	*Journal of Economic Behavior & Organization*	3	0
Cipriani et al.	June 2013	Like Mother Like Son? Experimental Evidence On The Transmission Of Values From Parents To Children	*Journal of Economic Behavior & Organization*	3	0
Prasad & Salmon	June 2013	Self Selection And Market Power In Risk Sharing Contracts	*Journal of Economic Behavior & Organization*	3	0
Chew et al.	June 2013	Sex-Hormone Genes And Gender Difference In Ultimatum Game: Experimental Evidence From China And Israel	*Journal of Economic Behavior & Organization*	3	2
Carlsson et al.	May 2013	The Truth, The Whole Truth, And Nothing But The Truth—A Multiple Country Test Of An Oath Script	*Journal of Economic Behavior & Organization*	3	1
Dietl et al.	May 2013	Incentive Effects Of Bonus Taxes In A Principal-Agent Model	*Journal of Economic Behavior & Organization*	3	0
Bucchianeri & Minson	May 2013	A Homeowner's Dilemma: Anchoring In Residential Real Estate Transactions	*Journal of Economic Behavior & Organization*	3	1
Finke & Huston	May 2013	Time Preference And The Importance Of Saving For Retirement	*Journal of Economic Behavior & Organization*	3	0
Kolmar & Rommeswinkel	May 2013	Contests With Group-Specific Public Goods And Complementarities In Efforts	*Journal of Economic Behavior & Organization*	3	1
Cartwright & Patel	Mar 2013	How Category Reporting Can Improve Fundraising	*Journal of Economic Behavior & Organization*	3	1
Crettez & Deloche	Mar 2013	On Experimental Economics And The Comparison Between The Last Two Versions Of Molière's Tartuffe	*Journal of Economic Behavior & Organization*	3	0

Authors	Date	Article title	Journal	Rank	Citations
Charness *et al.*	Mar 2013	Experimental Methods: Eliciting Risk Preferences	Journal of Economic Behavior & Organization	3	1
Ivanov *et al.*	Mar 2013	Behavioral Biases In Endogenous-Timing Herding Games: An Experimental Study	Journal of Economic Behavior & Organization	3	0
Lengnick	Feb 2013	Agent-Based Macroeconomics: A Baseline Model	Journal of Economic Behavior & Organization	3	0
Hyll & Schneider	Feb 2013	The Causal Effect Of Watching TV On Material Aspirations: Evidence From The "Valley Of The Innocent"	Journal of Economic Behavior & Organization	3	1
Sorger & Stark	Feb 2013	Income Redistribution Going Awry: The Reversal Power Of The Concern For Relative Deprivation	Journal of Economic Behavior & Organization	3	1
Parente & Winn	Nov 2012	Bargaining Behavior And The Tragedy Of The Anticommons	Journal of Economic Behavior & Organization	3	0
Papi	Sept 2012	Satisficing Choice Procedures	Journal of Economic Behavior & Organization	3	1
Glazer	Sept 2012	Up-Or-Out Policies When A Worker Imitates Another	Journal of Economic Behavior & Organization	3	0
Le Coq & Sturluson	Sept 2012	Does Opponents' Experience Matter? Experimental Evidence From A Quantity Precommitment Game	Journal of Economic Behavior & Organization	3	1
Zubrickas	Sept 2012	How Exposure To Markets Can Favor Inequity-Averse Preferences	Journal of Economic Behavior & Organization	3	0
Gurtler & Gurtler	Sept 2012	Inequality Aversion And Externalities	Journal of Economic Behavior & Organization	3	1
Lin & Rassenti	Sept 2012	Are Under- And Over-Reaction The Same Matter? Experimental Evidence	Journal of Economic Behavior & Organization	3	0

Authors	Date	Article title	Journal	Rank	Citations
Arango & Moxnes	Sept 2012	Commodity Cycles, A Function Of Market Complexity? Extending The Cobweb Experiment	*Journal of Economic Behavior & Organization*	3	1
Alos-Ferrer & Hugelschafer	Sept 2012	Faith In Intuition And Behavioral Biases	*Journal of Economic Behavior & Organization*	3	1
Giansante et al.	Aug 2012	Structural Contagion And Vulnerability To Unexpected Liquidity Shortfalls	*Journal of Economic Behavior & Organization*	3	1
Sordi & Vercelli	Aug 2012	Heterogeneous Expectations And Strong Uncertainty In A Minskyian Model Of Financial Fluctuations	*Journal of Economic Behavior & Organization*	3	0
Grajzl & Baniak	May 2012	Mandating Behavioral Conformity In Social Groups With Conformist Members	*Journal of Economic Behavior & Organization*	3	0
Conlisk	Apr 2011	Professor Zak's Empirical Studies On Trust And Oxytocin	*Journal of Economic Behavior & Organization*	3	1
Volk et al.	Feb 2012	Temporal Stability And Psychological Foundations Of Cooperation Preferences	*Journal of Economic Behavior & Organization*	3	3
Burns	Feb 2012	Race, Diversity And Pro-Social Behavior In A Segmented Society	*Journal of Economic Behavior & Organization*	3	0
Kocher et al.	Feb 2012	Social Background, Cooperative Behavior, And Norm Enforcement	*Journal of Economic Behavior & Organization*	3	0
Brousseau et al.	June 2011	Institutional Changes: Alternative Theories And Consequences For Institutional Design	*Journal of Economic Behavior & Organization*	3	0
Branas-Garza et al.	Apr 2011	Travelers' Types	*Journal of Economic Behavior & Organization*	3	2
Stringham	Apr 2011	Embracing Morals In Economics: The Role Of Internal Moral Constraints In A Market Economy	*Journal of Economic Behavior & Organization*	3	3

Authors	Date	Article title	Journal	Rank	Citations
Bucciol *et al.*	Apr 2011	Temptation And Productivity: A Field Experiment With Children	*Journal of Economic Behavior & Organization*	3	2
Huang	Apr 2011	Price-Taking Behavior Versus Continuous Dynamic Optimizing	*Journal of Economic Behavior & Organization*	3	0
Beshears & Milkman	Mar 2011	Do Sell-Side Stock Analysts Exhibit Escalation Of Commitment?	*Journal of Economic Behavior & Organization*	3	0
Fehr-Duda *et al.*	Apr 2011	Risk And Rationality: The Effects Of Mood And Decision Rules On Probability Weighting	*Journal of Economic Behavior & Organization*	3	2
McAlvanah	Nov 2010	Subadditivity, Patience, And Utility: The Effects Of Dividing Time Intervals	*Journal of Economic Behavior & Organization*	3	1
Binswanger	Nov 2010	Understanding The Heterogeneity Of Savings And Asset Allocation: A Behavioral-Economics Perspective	*Journal of Economic Behavior & Organization*	3	1
Oechssler *et al.*	Oct 2009	Cognitive Abilities And Behavioral Biases	*Journal of Economic Behavior & Organization*	3	15
Menkhoff & Nikiforow	Aug 2009	Professionals' Endorsement Of Behavioral Finance: Does It Impact Their Perception Of Markets And Themselves?	*Journal of Economic Behavior & Organization*	3	6
Gowdy	Dec 2008	Behavioral Economics And Climate Change Policy	*Journal of Economic Behavior & Organization*	3	8
Burnham	June 2013	Toward A Neo-Darwinian Synthesis Of Neoclassical And Behavioral Economics	*Journal of Economic Behavior & Organization*	3	1
Stoelhorst & Richerson	June 2013	A Naturalistic Theory Of Economic Organization	*Journal of Economic Behavior & Organization*	3	0
Wilson & Gowdy	June 2013	Evolution As A General Theoretical Framework For Economics And Public Policy	*Journal of Economic Behavior & Organization*	3	3

Authors	Date	Article title	Journal	Rank	Citations
Biglan & Cody	June 2013	Integrating The Human Sciences To Evolve Effective Policies	Journal of Economic Behavior & Organization	3	0
Mullins et al.	June 2013	The Role Of Writing And Recordkeeping In The Cultural Evolution Of Human Cooperation	Journal of Economic Behavior & Organization	3	0
Alevy et al.	Aug 2011	How Can Behavioral Economics Inform Nonmarket Valuation? An Example From The Preference Reversal Literature	Land Economics	3	0
Czajkowski	May 2009	Modeling Shifts In Willingness To Pay From A Bayesian Updating Perspective	Land Economics	3	1
Fenichel et al.	May 2009	Split-Sample Tests Of "No Opinion" Responses In An Attribute-Based Choice Model	Land Economics	3	0
Borowczyk-Martins et al.	July 2013	Accounting For Endogeneity In Matching Function Estimation	Review of Economic Dynamics	3	2
Tutino	July 2013	Rationally Inattentive Consumption Choices	Review of Economic Dynamics	3	0
Bayer & Juessen	July 2012	On The Dynamics Of Interstate Migration: Migration Costs And Self-Selection	Review of Economic Dynamics	3	1
Blackwell	Nov 2011	A Quasi-Experimental Test Of The Marginal Trader Hypothesis	Kyklos	3	0
Datta & Mullainathan	Mar 2014	Behavioral Design: A New Approach To Development Policy	Review of Income & Wealth	3	1
D'Exelle & van den Berg	Mar 2014	Aid Distribution And Cooperation In Unequal Communities	Review of Income & Wealth	3	1
Jantti et al.	Mar 2014	Poverty, Development, And Behavioral Economics	Review of Income & Wealth	3	0

Authors	Date	Article title	Journal	Rank	Citations
Luebker	Mar 2014	Income Inequality, Redistribution, And Poverty: Contrasting Rational Choice And Behavioral Perspectives	*Review of Income & Wealth*	3	1
Gunther & Maier	Mar 2014	Poverty, Vulnerability, And Reference-Dependent Utility	*Review of Income & Wealth*	3	1
Jantti *et al.*	Mar 2014	Poverty And Welfare Measurement On The Basis Of Prospect Theory	*Review of Income & Wealth*	3	2
Dow	Jan 2015	Addressing Uncertainty In Economics And The Economy	*Cambridge Journal of Economics*	3	0
Wrede	July 2011	Hyperbolic Discounting And Fertility	*Journal of Population Economics*	3	0
Averett *et al.*	July 2011	Older Siblings And Adolescent Risky Behavior: Does Parenting Play A Role?	*Journal of Population Economics*	3	0
Backhouse & Medema	Oct 2009	Defining Economics: The Long Road To Acceptance Of The Robbins Definition	*Economica*	3	4
Hands	Oct 2009	Effective Tension In Robbins' Economic Methodology	*Economica*	3	2
Sugden	Oct 2009	Can Economics Be Founded On 'Indisputable Facts Of Experience'? Lionel Robbins And The Pioneers Of Neoclassical Economics	*Economica*	3	0
Atkinson	Oct 2009	Economics As A Moral Science	*Economica*	3	5
Campbell	July 2014	Empirical Asset Pricing: Eugene Fama, Lars Peter Hansen, And Robert Shiller	*Scandinavian Journal of Economics*	3	0
Kanbur *et al.*	July 2008	Moral Hazard, Income Taxation And Prospect Theory	*Scandinavian Journal of Economics*	3	3

Authors	Date	Article title	Journal	Rank	Citations
Hadjiyiannis et al.	Aug 2012	Multilateral Tariff Cooperation Under Fairness And Reciprocity	Canadian Journal of Economics	3	0
Kalaitzidakis et al.	Nov 2011	An Updated Ranking Of Academic Journals In Economics	Canadian Journal of Economics	3	4
Corrigan et al.	Apr 2014	Do Practice Rounds Affect Experimental Auction Results?	Economics Letters	3	0
Linder & Sutter	Sept 2013	Level- Reasoning And Time Pressure In The 11–20 Money Request Game	Economics Letters	3	0
Godoy et al.	Sept 2013	Competition Lessens Competition: An Experimental Investigation Of Simultaneous Participation In A Public Good Game And A Lottery Contest Game With Shared Endowment			
Riener & Wiederhold	Sept 2013	Heterogeneous Treatment Effects In Groups	Economics Letters	3	0
Di Guida et al.	Dec 2012	Decisions Among Defaults And The Effect Of The Option To Do Nothing	Economics Letters	3	0
Gallardo	Sept 2013	Using The Downside Mean-Semideviation For Measuring Vulnerability To Poverty	Economics Letters	3	0
Kaivanto & Kroll	May 2012	Negative Recency, Randomization Device Choice, And Reduction Of Compound Lotteries	Economics Letters	3	0
Morone	Feb 2012	A Simple Model Of Herd Behavior, A Comment	Economics Letters	3	1
Weber	Jan 2012	An Augmented Becker–Degroot–Marschak Mechanism For Transaction Cycles	Economics Letters	3	0
Aronsson & Granlund	Oct 2011	Public Goods And Optimal Paternalism Under Present-Biased Preferences	Economics Letters	3	0
Zizzo & Fleming	June 2011	Can Experimental Measures Of Sensitivity To Social Pressure Predict Public Good Contribution?	Economics Letters	3	3

Authors	Date	Article title	Journal	Rank	Citations
Bettin et al.	May 2012	Financial Development And Remittances: Micro-Econometric Evidence	Economics Letters	3	0
Immordino et al.	Dec 2011	A Simple Impossibility Result In Behavioral Contract Theory	Economics Letters	3	1
Gwilym	Aug 2010	Can Behavioral Finance Models Account For Historical Asset Prices?	Economics Letters	3	1
McQuillin & Sugden	Apr 2012	Reconciling Normative And Behavioural Economics: The Problems To Be Solved	Social Choice & Welfare	2	1
McQuillin & Sugden	Apr 2012	How The Market Responds To Dynamically Inconsistent Preferences	Social Choice & Welfare	2	1
Qizilbash	Apr 2012	Informed Desire And The Ambitions Of Libertarian Paternalism	Social Choice & Welfare	2	3
Sandbu	Dec 2008	Axiomatic Foundations For Fairness-Motivated Preferences	Social Choice & Welfare	2	2
Hudik	Dec 2014	Reference-Dependence And Marginal Utility: Alt, Samuelson, And Bernardelli	History of Political Economy	2	0
Rancan	Mar 2013	Modigliani's And Simon's Early Contributions To Uncertainty (1952-61)	History of Political Economy	2	0
Edwards	Dec 2012	Observing Attitudes, Intentions, And Expectations (1945–73)	History of Political Economy	2	0
Heukelom	Dec 2011	What To Conclude From Psychological Experiments: The Contrasting Cases Of Experimental And Behavioral Economics	History of Political Economy	2	1
Bateman	June 2011	In A Space Of Questions: A Reflection On Religion And Economics At The Beginning Of The Twenty-First Century	History of Political Economy	2	0
Pooley & Solovey	Dec 2010	Marginal To The Revolution: The Curious Relationship Between Economics And The Behavioral Sciences Movement In Mid-Twentieth-Century America	History of Political Economy	2	1

Authors	Date	Article title	Journal	Rank	Citations
Nomikos & Andriosopoulos	July 2012	Modelling Energy Spot Prices: Empirical Evidence From NYMEX	*Energy Economics*	2	2
Dagher	July 2012	Natural Gas Demand At The Utility Level: An Application Of Dynamic Elasticities	*Energy Economics*	2	2
Breton & Kharbach	July 2012	Transportation And Storage Under A Dynamic Price Cap Regulation Process	*Energy Economics*	2	0
Van der Veen *et al.*	July 2012	Agent-Based Analysis Of The Impact Of The Imbalance Pricing Mechanism On Market Behavior In Electricity Balancing Markets	*Energy Economics*	2	0
Boeters & Bollen	Dec 2012	Fossil Fuel Supply, Leakage And The Effectiveness Of Border Measures In Climate Policy	*Energy Economics*	2	1
Binder	July 2014	Should Evolutionary Economists Embrace Libertarian Paternalism?	*Journal of Evolutionary Economics*	2	3
Beckenbach *et al.*	July 2012	Agent-Based Modelling Of Novelty Creating Behavior And Sectoral Growth Effects-Linking The Creative And The Destructive Side Of Innovation	*Journal of Evolutionary Economics*	2	0
Berninghaus *et al.*	Oct 2007	Reciprocity—An Indirect Evolutionary Analysis	*Journal of Evolutionary Economics*	2	2
Cherry *et al.*	Nov 2014	The Impact Of Trial Runs On The Acceptability Of Environmental Taxes: Experimental Evidence	*Resource & Energy Economics*	2	0
Lusk	July 2014	Are You Smart Enough To Know What To Eat? A Critique Of Behavioural Economics As Justification For Regulation	*European Review of Agricultural Economics*	2	0
Huijps *et al.*	Dec 2010	Sub-Optimal Economic Behaviour With Respect To Mastitis Management	*European Review of Agricultural Economics*	2	0

Authors	Date	Article title	Journal	Rank	Citations
Delaney *et al.*	Feb 2013	The Role Of Noncognitive Traits In Undergraduate Study Behaviours	*Economics of Education Review*	2	0
Mayraz	Dec 2014	A Course In Behavioral Economics	*Economic Record*	2	0
Hashimzade *et al.*	Dec 2013	Applications Of Behavioural Economics To Tax Evasion	*Journal of Economic Surveys*	2	1
Rassenfosse & van Pottelsberghe de la Potterie	Sept 2013	The Role Of Fees In Patent Systems: Theory And Evidence	*Journal of Economic Surveys*	2	0
Garcia	Apr 2013	Financial Education And Behavioral Finance: New Insights Into The Role Of Information In Financial Decisions	*Journal of Economic Surveys*	2	0
Willemien	Dec 2012	Learning With Fixed Rules: The Minority Game	*Journal of Economic Surveys*	2	0
Festr	July 2010	Incentives And Social Norms: A Motivation-Based Economic Analysis Of Social Norms	*Journal of Economic Surveys*	2	1
Lines & Westerhoff	Oct 2012	Effects Of Inflation Expectations On Macroeconomic Dynamics: Extrapolative Versus Regressive Expectations	*Studies in Nonlinear Dynamics & Econometrics*	2	0
Anufriev & Giulio	Oct 2012	Asset Pricing With Heterogeneous Investment Horizons	*Studies in Nonlinear Dynamics & Econometrics*	2	0
Wymer	Apr 2012	Continuous-Time Econometrics Of Structural Models	*Studies in Nonlinear Dynamics & Econometrics*	2	0
Brekke & Johansson-Stenman	Aug 2008	The Behavioural Economics Of Climate Change	*Oxford Review of Economic Policy*	2	15
Cooper & Kovacic	Feb 2012	Behavioral Economics: Implications For Regulatory Behavior	*Journal of Regulatory Economics*	2	3
Driscoll & Holden	Sept 2014	Behavioral Economics And Macroeconomic Models	*Journal of Macroeconomics*	2	0
Hoover & Young	July 2013	Rational Expectations: Retrospect And Prospect	*Macroeconomic Dynamics*	2	0

Authors	Date	Article title	Journal	Rank	Citations
Bogan et al.	July 2013	Do Psychological Shocks Affect Financial Risk Taking Behavior? A Study Of U.S. Veterans	Contemporary Economic Policy	2	0
Wong	Oct 2012	Consumption Response To Government Transfers: Behavioral Motives Revealed By Savers And Spenders	Contemporary Economic Policy	2	0
Xie & Yang	Jan 2015	Investor Sentiment And The Financial Crisis: A Sentiment-Based Portfolio Theory Perspective	Applied Economics	2	0
Claar et al.	July 2013	Spreading Academic Pay Over Nine Or Twelve Months: Economists Are Supposed To Know Better, But Do They Act Better?	Applied Economics	2	0
Dobbs & Miller	June 2014	Inducing Risk Preferences In Multi-Stage Multi-Agent Laboratory Experiments	Applied Economics	2	0
Weng & Yang	June 2014	The Impact Of Social Identity On Trust In China: Experimental Evidence From Cross-Group Comparisons	Applied Economics	2	0
Azar	Mar 2013	Firm Strategy And Biased Decision Making: The Price Dispersion Puzzle	Applied Economics	2	0
Bellani et al.	Sept 2013	Multidimensional Welfare: Do Groups Vary In Their Priorities And Behaviours?	Fiscal Studies	2	0
Hillman	Dec 2010	Expressive Behavior In Economics And Politics	European Journal of Political Economy	2	2
Lai	Feb 2012	Shock-Dependent Conditional Skewness In International Aggregate Stock Markets	Quarterly Review of Economics & Finance	2	0
Depken & Zhang	Nov 2010	Adverse Selection And Reputation In A World Of Cheap Talk	Quarterly Review of Economics & Finance	2	0
Elze	Nov 2010	Value Investing Anomalies In The European Stock Market: Multiple Value, Consistent Earner, And Recognized Value	Quarterly Review of Economics & Finance	2	0

Authors	Date	Article title	Journal	Rank	Citations
Hands	Dec 2014	Normative Ecological Rationality: Normative Rationality In The Fast-And-Frugal-Heuristics Research Program	Journal of Economic Methodology	2	0
Berg	Dec 2014	The Consistency And Ecological Rationality Approaches To Normative Bounded Rationality	Journal of Economic Methodology	2	0
Jullien & Vallois	Sept 2014	A Probabilistic Ghost In The Experimental Machine	Journal of Economic Methodology	2	1
Edwards	Dec 2012	The History Of The Use Of Self-Reports And The Methodology Of Economics	Journal of Economic Methodology	2	0
Ross	Dec 2010	Should The Financial Crisis Inspire Normative Revision?	Journal of Economic Methodology	2	0
Plott et al.	Oct 2011	Introduction To The Special Issue On Behavioral And Experimental Public Economics	Journal of Public Economic Theory	2	0
Hasson et al.	Sept 2012	Treatment Effects Of Climate Change Risk On Mitigation And Adaptation Behaviour In An Experimental Setting	South African Journal of Economics	1	0
Golikova et al.	June 2012	Does International Trade Provide Incentives For Efficient Behaviour Of Russian Manufacturing Firms?	Post-Communist Economies	1	1
Huston & Spencer	Feb 2014	Housing And Behavioural Factors	Applied Economics Letters	1	0
Kang & Kim	Mar 2012	An Interrelation Of Time Preference And Risk Attitude: An Application To The Equity Premium Puzzle	Applied Economics Letters	1	0
Yoon	Sept 2013	Common Change-Points In Long-Term UK Bond Yields, 1870–1914: A Piecewise Linear Trends Approach	Applied Economics Letters	1	0
Fusaro & Dutkowsky	Sept 2013	What Explains Consumption And Money Holding In The Very Short-Run?: Evidence From Checking Account Data	Applied Economics Letters	1	0

Authors	Date	Article title	Journal	Rank	Citations
Wu & Wang	Aug 2011	The Relationships Between Rent Multiplier And User Cost – A Case Study Of Taipei	*Applied Economics Letters*	1	0
Earl & Peng	July 2012	Brands Of Economics And The Trojan Horse Of Pluralism	*Review of Political Economy*	1	0
Hands	May 2011	Back To The Ordinalist Revolution: Behavioral Economic Concerns In Early Modern Consumer Choice Theory	*Metroeconomica*	1	3

Appendix 3.1 Bounded rationality

Primary articles

Authors	Date	Article title	Journal	Rank	Citations
Rubinstein & Salant	Jan 2012	Eliciting Welfare Preferences From Behavioural Data Sets	Review of Economic Studies	4	6
Eliaz & Spiegler	Jan 2011	Consideration Sets And Competitive Marketing	Review of Economic Studies	4	12
Wilson	Nov 2014	Bounded Memory And Biases In Information Processing	Econometrica	4	0
Manzini & Mariotti	May 2014	Stochastic Choice And Consideration Sets	Econometrica	4	3
	Jan 2009	Two New Conditions Supporting The First-Order Approach To Multisignal Principal-Agent Problems	Econometrica	4	6
	Jan 2009	The Complexity Of Forecast Testing	Econometrica	4	4
Siegel	Jan 2009	All-Pay Contests	Econometrica	4	22
Govindan & Wilson	Jan 2009	On Forward Induction	Econometrica	4	2
De Clippel & Serrano	Nov 2008	Marginal Contributions And Externalities In The Value	Econometrica	4	8
Blundell et al.	Nov 2008	Best Nonparametric Bounds On Demand Responses	Econometrica	4	14
Fehr & Tyran	Mar 2008	Limited Rationality And Strategic Interaction: The Impact Of The Strategic Environment On Nominal Inertia	Econometrica	4	17
Crawford & Iriberri	Nov 2007	Level-K Auctions: Can A Nonequilibrium Model Of Strategic Thinking Explain The Winner's Curse And Overbidding In Private-Value Auctions?	Econometrica	4	34
Smeulders et al.	Dec 2013	The Money Pump As A Measure Of Revealed Preference Violations: A Comment	Journal of Political Economy	4	0
Glazer & Rubinstein	Dec 2012	A Model Of Persuasion With Boundedly Rational Agents	Journal of Political Economy	4	2
Brown et al.	Feb 2009	Learning And Visceral Temptation In Dynamic Saving Experiments	Quarterly Journal of Economics	4	10
Bernheim & Rangel	Feb 2009	Beyond Revealed Preference: Choice-Theoretic Foundations For Behavioral Welfare Economics	Quarterly Journal of Economics	4	22
Arad & Rubinstein	Dec 2012	The 11–20 Money Request Game: A Level-K Reasoning Study	American Economic Review	4	2

Authors	Date	Article title	Journal	Rank	Citations
Masatlioglu *et al.*	Aug 2012	Revealed Attention	American Economic Review	4	8
Lacetera *et al.*	Aug 2012	Heuristic Thinking And Limited Attention In The Car Market	American Economic Review	4	5
Matejka & McKay	May 2012	Simple Market Equilibria With Rationally Inattentive Consumers	American Economic Review	4	1
Mackowiak & Wiederholt	May 2012	Information Processing And Limited Liability	American Economic Review	4	0
Salant	Apr 2011	Procedural Analysis Of Choice Rules With Applications To Bounded Rationality	American Economic Review	4	3
Rabin & Weizsacker	Sept 2009	Narrow Bracketing And Dominated Choices	American Economic Review	4	12
Tirole	Mar 2009	Cognition And Incomplete Contracts	American Economic Review	4	23
Manzini & Mariotti	Dec 2007	Sequentially Rationalizable Choice	American Economic Review	4	35
Harstad & Selten	June 2013	Bounded-Rationality Models: Tasks To Become Intellectually Competitive	Journal of Economic Literature	4	2
Rabin	June 2013	Incorporating Limited Rationality Into Economics	Journal of Economic Literature	4	1
Crawford	June 2013	Boundedly Rational Versus Optimization-Based Models Of Strategic Thinking And Learning In Games	Journal of Economic Literature	4	1
Halpern & Pass	Mar 2015	Algorithmic Rationality: Game Theory With Costly Computation	Journal of Economic Theory	4	0
Golman	Sept 2011	Quantal Response Equilibria With Heterogeneous Agents	Journal of Economic Theory	4	2
Liu	Sept 2009	On Redundant Types And Bayesian Formulation Of Incomplete Information	Journal of Economic Theory	4	2
Rogers *et al.*	July 2009	Heterogeneous Quantal Response Equilibrium And Cognitive Hierarchies	Journal of Economic Theory	4	11

Authors	Date	Article title	Journal	Rank	Citations
Tyson	Jan 2008	Cognitive Constraints, Contraction Consistency, And The Satisficing Criterion	Journal of Economic Theory	4	4
Krasa & Gruner	May 2007	Limited Observability As A Constraint In Contract Design	Journal of Economic Theory	4	1
Schulte & Gruner	May 2007	Speed And Quality Of Collective Decision Making: Imperfect Information Processing	Journal of Economic Theory	4	2
Miravete & Palacios-Huerta	July 2014	Consumer Inertia, Choice Dependence, And Learning From Experience In A Repeated Decision Problem	Review of Economics and Statistics	4	1
Lundberg & Pollak	Mar 2007	The American Family And Family Economics	Journal of Economic Perspectives	4	10
Sarafidis	Mar 2007	What Have You Done For Me Lately? Release Of Information And Strategic Manipulation Of Memories	The Economic Journal	4	6
Bruni & Sugden	Jan 2007	The Road Not Taken: How Psychology Was Removed From Economics, And How It Might Be Brought Back	The Economic Journal	4	24
Camerer	Mar 2007	Neuroeconomics: Using Neuroscience To Make Economic Predictions	The Economic Journal	4	13
Corazzini et al.	Aug 2012	Influential Listeners: An Experiment On Persuasion Bias In Social Networks	European Economic Review	3	1
Binswanger	Apr 2012	Life Cycle Saving: Insights From The Perspective Of Bounded Rationality	European Economic Review	3	0
Miao	Oct 2010	Consumer Myopia, Standardization And Aftermarket Monopolization	European Economic Review	3	1
Burton & Rigby	Apr 2012	The Self Selection Of Complexity In Choice Experiments	American Journal of Agricultural Economics	3	0
Eliaz & Rubinstein	Nov 2014	A Model Of Boundedly Rational 'Neuro' Agents	Economic Theory	3	0

Authors	Date	Article title	Journal	Rank	Citations
Grant & Quiggin	Nov 2013	Inductive Reasoning About Unawareness	Economic Theory	3	0
Reise et al.	Jan 2012	Which Factors Influence The Expansion Of Bioenergy? An Empirical Study Of The Investment Behaviours Of German Farmers	Ecological Economics	3	1
Chen & Zhang	Nov 2011	Equilibrium Price Dispersion With Heterogeneous Searchers	International Journal of Industrial Organization	3	1
Kalayci & Potters	Jan 2011	Buyer Confusion And Market Prices	International Journal of Industrial Organization	3	0
Yao & Li	Jan 2013	Bounded Rationality As A Source Of Loss Aversion And Optimism: A Study Of Psychological Adaptation Under Incomplete Information	Journal of Economic Dynamics & Control	3	2
Fazzari et al.	Oct 2010	Investment And The Taylor Rule In A Dynamic Keynesian Model	Journal of Economic Dynamics & Control	3	0
Arifovic et al.	Sept 2010	Learning Benevolent Leadership In A Heterogenous Agents Economy	Journal of Economic Dynamics & Control	3	0
Schipper	Dec 2009	Imitators And Optimizers In Cournot Oligopoly	Journal of Economic Dynamics & Control	3	3
Colomer	Mar 2014	Equilibrium Institutions: The Federal-Proportional Trade-Off	Public Choice	3	0
Buchanan & Yoon	Oct 2012	Choosing For Others: A Neglected Element In The Theory Of Collective Action	Public Choice	3	0
Demuynck	Aug 2011	The Computational Complexity Of Rationalizing Boundedly Rational Choice Behavior	Journal of Mathematical Economics	3	0
Gerasimou	Sept 2010	Consumer Theory With Bounded Rational Preferences	Journal of Mathematical Economics	3	0

Authors	Date	Article title	Journal	Rank	Citations
Manea	Sept 2008	Unique Induced Preference Representations	*Journal of Mathematical Economics*	3	0
Markiewicz *et al.*	Nov 2014	Adaptive Learning And Survey Data	*Journal of Economic Behavior & Organization*	3	0
Lim *et al.*	Mar 2014	Bounded Rationality And Group Size In Tullock Contests: Experimental Evidence	*Journal of Economic Behavior & Organization*	3	1
Le Coq & Sturluson	Sept 2012	Does Opponents' Experience Matter? Experimental Evidence From A Quantity Precommitment Game	*Journal of Economic Behavior & Organization*	3	1
Golman	Apr 2012	Homogeneity Bias In Models Of Discrete Choice With Bounded Rationality	*Journal of Economic Behavior & Organization*	3	1
Szech	Sept 2011	Becoming A Bad Doctor	*Journal of Economic Behavior & Organization*	3	1
Feigenbaum *et al.*	Mar 2011	Optimal Irrational Behavior	*Journal of Economic Behavior & Organization*	3	2
Binswanger	Nov 2010	Understanding The Heterogeneity Of Savings And Asset Allocation: A Behavioral-Economics Perspective	*Journal of Economic Behavior & Organization*	3	1
Corgnet *et al.*	Nov 2010	The Effect Of Reliability, Content And Timing Of Public Announcements On Asset Trading Behavior	*Journal of Economic Behavior & Organization*	3	1
Guth	Mar 2010	Satisficing And (Un)Bounded Rationality: A Formal Definition And Its Experimental Validity	*Journal of Economic Behavior & Organization*	3	0
Dohmen *et al.*	Dec 2009	Biased Probability Judgment: Evidence Of Incidence And Relationship To Economic Outcomes From A Representative Sample	*Journal of Economic Behavior & Organization*	3	3

Authors	Date	Article title	Journal	Rank	Citations
Fenichel *et al.*	May 2009	Split-Sample Tests Of "No Opinion" Responses In An Attribute-Based Choice Model	*Land Economics*	3	0
Botzen *et al.*	May 2009	Bounded Rationality, Climate Risks, And Insurance: Is There A Market For Natural Disasters?	*Land Economics*	3	2
Colombo & Hanley	Feb 2008	How Can We Reduce The Errors From Benefits Transfer? An Investigation Using The Choice Experiment Method	*Land Economics*	3	1
Bateman *et al.*	Feb 2008	Decoy Effects In Choice Experiments And Contingent Valuation: Asymmetric Dominance	*Land Economics*	3	4
Mehta	Nov 2013	The Discourse Of Bounded Rationality In Academic And Policy Arenas: Pathologising The Errant Consumer	*Cambridge Journal of Economics*	3	0
Carrion-i-Silvestre & Gadea	Aug 2013	GLS-Based Unit Root Tests For Bounded Processes	*Economics Letters*	3	0
Jerger & Michaelis	Feb 2011	The Fixed Wage Puzzle: Why Profit Sharing Is So Hard To Implement	*Economics Letters*	3	0
Miettinen	Nov 2009	The Partially Cursed And The Analogy-Based Expectation Equilibrium	*Economics Letters*	3	1
Weirich	Dec 2007	Collective, Universal, And Joint Rationality	*Social Choice & Welfare*	2	0
Ioannou	July 2014	Coevolution Of Finite Automata With Errors	*Journal of Evolutionary Economics*	2	0
Valente	Nov 2012	Evolutionary Demand: A Model For Boundedly Rational Consumers	*Journal of Evolutionary Economics*	2	2
Mallard	Sept 2012	Modelling Cognitively Bounded Rationality: An Evaluative Taxonomy	*Journal of Economic Surveys*	2	4
Sarukkai	July 2011	Complexity And Randomness In Mathematics: hilosophical Reflections On The Relevance For Economic Modelling	*Journal of Economic Surveys*	2	0

Authors	Date	Article title	Journal	Rank	Citations
Lee	July 2011	Bounded Rationality And The Emergence Of Simplicity Amidst Complexity	Journal of Economic Surveys	2	2
Bullard et al.	Apr 2010	A Model Of Near-Rational Exuberance	Macroeconomic Dynamics	2	2
Yu & Yu	Feb 2014	A Dynamic Duopoly Model With Bounded Rationality Based On Constant Conjectural Variation	Economic Modelling	2	0
Ferreiro & Serrano	Mar 2012	Expectations, Uncertainty And Institutions. An Application To The Analysis Of Social Security Reforms	International Review of Applied Economics	2	0
Binswanger & Prufer	Sept 2012	Democracy, Populism, And (Un)Bounded Rationality	European Journal of Political Economy	2	0
Grune-Yanoff et al.	Dec 2014	Introduction: Methodologies Of Bounded Rationality	Journal of Economic Methodology	2	0
Berg	Dec 2014	The Consistency And Ecological Rationality Approaches To Normative Bounded Rationality	Journal of Economic Methodology	2	0
Ross	Dec 2014	Psychological Versus Economic Models Of Bounded Rationality	Journal of Economic Methodology	2	0
Manzini & Mariotti	Dec 2014	Welfare Economics And Bounded Rationality: The Case For Model-Based Approaches	Journal of Economic Methodology	2	0
Katsikopoulos	Dec 2014	Bounded Rationality: The Two Cultures	Journal of Economic Methodology	2	0
Fiori	Sept 2009	Hayek's Theory On Complexity And Knowledge: Dichotomies, Levels Of Analysis, And Bounded Rationality	Journal of Economic Methodology	2	0
Fiori	Oct 2011	Forms Of Bounded Rationality: The Reception And Redefinition Of Herbert A. Simon's Perspective	Review of Political Economy	1	0

Appendix 4.1 Dataset

Observation	logCitations	Rank	Time	Category
1	1.791759	4	37	0
2	2.484907	4	49	0
3	–	4	4	0
4	1.098612	4	10	0
5	1.791759	4	73	0
6	1.386294	4	73	0
7	3.091043	4	73	0
8	0.693147	4	73	0
9	2.079442	4	76	0
10	2.639057	4	76	0
11	2.833213	4	83	0
12	1.609438	4	37	1
13	1.609438	4	73	1
14	3.091043	4	73	1
15	0.693147	4	73	1
16	1.609438	4	76	1
17	2.079442	4	76	1
18	2.890372	4	76	1
19	2.639057	4	76	1
20	1.791759	4	73	1
21	1.386294	4	73	1
22	–	4	73	1
23	–	4	15	0
24	0.693147	4	27	0
25	2.70805	4	70	1
26	2.302585	4	72	1
27	3.091043	4	72	1
28	2.302585	4	72	0
29	3.091043	4	72	0
30	0.693147	4	27	0
31	2.079442	4	31	0
32	1.609438	4	31	0
33	0	4	34	0
34	–	4	34	0
35	1.098612	4	47	0

Observation	logCitations	Rank	Time	Category
36	2.484907	4	66	0
37	3.135494	4	71	0
38	–	4	5	1
39	–	4	9	1
40	–	4	46	1
41	1.098612	4	47	1
42	0	4	22	1
43	–	4	22	1
44	1.94591	4	78	1
45	0.693147	4	94	1
46	0	4	21	1
47	0.693147	4	21	0
48	0	4	21	0
49	0	4	21	0
50	–	4	25	1
51	1.386294	4	34	1
52	0.693147	4	42	0
53	0.693147	4	66	0
54	2.397895	4	68	0
55	1.386294	4	85	0
56	0	4	94	0
57	0.693147	4	94	0
58	–	4	28	1
59	0.693147	4	28	1
60	0	4	32	1
61	–	4	5	1
62	–	4	17	1
63	0	4	8	1
64	0	4	8	0
65	1.609438	4	64	1
66	–	4	9	1
67	1.609438	4	15	1
68	2.484907	4	42	1
69	2.70805	4	39	1
70	0	4	39	1
71	1.098612	4	39	1
72	1.609438	4	81	1
73	3.135494	4	117	1
74	2.302585	4	95	0
75	1.791759	4	95	0
76	3.178054	4	97	0
77	2.564949	4	95	0
78	–	4	9	1
79	0	4	73	1
80	3.258096	4	89	1
81	–	4	28	1
82	1.098612	4	44	1
83	–	4	28	1

Observation	logCitations	Rank	Time	Category
84	0.693147	4	75	1
85	1.098612	3	28	1
86	0.693147	3	28	1
87	1.098612	3	36	1
88	0	3	31	0
89	–	3	35	0
90	0	3	53	0
91	–	3	1	1
92	–	3	10	1
93	0.693147	3	51	1
94	–	3	10	1
95	–	3	35	0
96	–	3	36	1
97	–	3	36	1
98	0.693147	3	67	1
99	–	3	4	0
100	–	3	16	0
101	0	3	37	0
102	–	3	6	1
103	–	3	6	1
104	0	3	40	0
105	–	3	49	0
106	0.693147	3	22	1
107	–	3	5	1
108	0.693147	3	25	0
109	–	3	53	0
110	–	3	54	0
111	1.098612	3	63	0
112	0	3	25	1
113	1.791759	3	52	1
114	–	3	11	0
115	–	3	29	0
116	–	3	43	0
117	–	3	54	0
118	–	3	78	0
119	0.693147	3	73	1
120	–	3	78	1
121	–	3	4	0
122	0	3	11	0
123	0	3	30	0
124	0	3	35	0
125	0	3	42	0
126	0.693147	3	47	0
127	0	3	52	0
128	0	3	52	0
129	–	3	59	0
130	1.098612	3	63	0
131	–	3	4	1

Observation	logCitations	Rank	Time	Category
132	–	3	4	1
133	–	3	4	1
134	–	3	4	1
135	–	3	13	1
136	–	3	13	1
137	–	3	13	1
138	–	3	13	1
139	–	3	20	1
140	–	3	13	1
141	–	3	21	1
142	–	3	21	1
143	0.693147	3	17	1
144	–	3	17	1
145	–	3	17	1
146	–	3	17	1
147	–	3	17	1
148	0.693147	3	17	1
149	–	3	17	1
150	1.098612	3	18	1
151	–	3	18	1
152	0	3	18	1
153	0	3	18	1
154	0	3	20	1
155	–	3	20	1
156	–	3	20	1
157	–	3	21	1
158	–	3	21	1
159	0.693147	3	21	1
160	0	3	21	1
161	0	3	21	1
162	–	3	20	1
163	0.693147	3	20	1
164	–	3	20	1
165	–	3	20	1
166	–	3	20	1
167	–	3	21	1
168	–	3	21	1
169	–	3	21	1
170	0.693147	3	21	1
171	0	3	22	1
172	–	3	22	1
173	0	3	22	1
174	–	3	22	1
175	0	3	22	1
176	0	3	23	1
177	–	3	23	1
178	0	3	23	1
179	–	3	23	1

Observation	logCitations	Rank	Time	Category
180	–	3	24	1
181	0	3	24	1
182	0	3	24	1
183	–	3	28	1
184	0	3	30	1
185	–	3	30	1
186	0	3	30	1
187	–	3	30	1
188	0	3	30	1
189	–	3	30	1
190	0	3	30	1
191	0	3	30	1
192	0	3	31	1
193	–	3	31	1
194	–	3	34	1
195	0	3	47	1
196	1.098612	3	36	1
197	–	3	36	1
198	–	3	36	1
199	–	3	45	1
200	0.693147	3	47	1
201	1.098612	3	47	1
202	0.693147	3	47	1
203	–	3	47	1
204	–	3	47	1
205	0.693147	3	47	1
206	0	3	52	1
207	0	3	52	1
208	2.70805	3	65	1
209	1.791759	3	67	1
210	2.079442	3	75	1
211	0	3	21	1
212	–	3	21	1
213	1.098612	3	21	1
214	–	3	21	1
215	–	3	21	1
216	–	3	70	0
217	0.693147	3	70	0
218	0	3	84	0
219	1.386294	3	84	0
220	–	3	43	1
221	0	3	70	1
222	–	3	70	1
223	0.693147	3	20	1
224	–	3	20	1
225	0	3	32	1
226	–	3	40	1
227	0	3	11	1

Observation	logCitations	Rank	Time	Category
228	0	3	11	1
229	–	3	11	1
230	0	3	11	1
231	0	3	11	1
232	0.693147	3	11	1
233	–	3	16	0
234	–	3	1	1
235	–	3	44	1
236	–	3	44	1
237	1.386294	3	65	1
238	0.693147	3	65	1
239	–	3	65	1
240	1.609438	3	65	1
241	–	3	8	1
242	1.098612	3	80	1
243	–	3	31	1
244	1.386294	3	40	1
245	–	3	19	0
246	–	3	48	0
247	0	3	64	0
248	–	3	11	1
249	–	3	18	1
250	–	3	18	1
251	–	3	18	1
252	–	3	27	1
253	–	3	18	1
254	–	3	34	1
255	0	3	36	1
256	–	3	37	1
257	–	3	41	1
258	1.098612	3	45	1
259	–	3	34	1
260	0	3	39	1
261	0	3	55	1
262	–	2	87	0
263	0	2	35	1
264	0	2	35	1
265	1.098612	2	35	1
266	0.693147	2	75	1
267	–	2	3	1
268	–	2	23	1
269	–	2	27	1
270	0	2	39	1
271	–	2	45	1
272	0	2	51	1
273	0.693147	2	32	1
274	0.693147	2	32	1
275	–	2	32	1

Observation	logCitations	Rank	Time	Category
276	–	2	32	1
277	0	2	27	1
278	–	2	8	0
279	0.693147	2	28	0
280	1.098612	2	8	1
281	–	2	32	1
282	0.693147	2	89	1
283	–	2	4	1
284	–	2	8	1
285	–	2	51	1
286	–	2	24	1
287	–	2	3	1
288	1.386294	2	30	0
289	–	2	44	0
290	0.693147	2	44	0
291	0	2	15	1
292	–	2	18	1
293	–	2	23	1
294	–	2	27	1
295	0	2	56	1
296	–	2	29	1
297	–	2	29	1
298	–	2	35	1
299	2.70805	2	79	1
300	1.098612	2	36	1
301	–	2	6	1
302	0.693147	2	59	0
303	–	2	20	1
304	–	2	20	1
305	–	2	29	1
306	–	2	1	1
307	–	2	20	1
308	–	2	9	1
309	–	2	9	1
310	–	2	23	1
311	–	2	12	0
312	–	2	18	1
313	–	2	35	0
314	–	2	30	0
315	0.693147	2	51	1
316	–	2	36	1
317	–	2	52	1
318	–	2	52	1
319	–	2	3	0
320	–	2	3	0
321	–	2	3	0
322	–	2	3	0
323	–	2	3	0

Observation	logCitations	Rank	Time	Category
324	–	2	66	0
325	–	2	3	1
326	–	2	3	1
327	0	2	6	1
328	–	2	27	1
329	–	2	51	1
330	–	2	41	1
331	–	1	30	1
332	0	1	33	1
333	–	1	12	1
334	–	1	35	1
335	–	1	18	1
336	–	1	18	1
337	–	1	43	1
338	–	1	41	0
339	–	1	32	1
340	1.098612	1	46	1
341	3.526361	4	88	0
342	3.526361	4	76	1
343	3.583519	4	70	1
344	3.555348	4	87	0

Appendix 6.1 Proofs of propositions

Proposition 1

For a linear MR_{PD}^{-1} curve, a change in the value of α is accompanied by a proportionally equal change in the value of β because $\beta = \alpha/\pi_{PD(OPT)}$ a change to α of $\alpha\lambda$ causes a change to β of $\alpha\lambda/\pi_{PD(OPT)}$ where λ is the proportional change in α.

Consider the case where the individual is satisficing, meaning the equilibrium between the MR_{PD}^{-1} and MR_{RE} curves is on the upward-sloping section of the MR_{RE} curve. For an increase in α to have no effect on the efficient allocation of the cognitive resource to this decision (and so $\pi^*_{PD1} = \pi^*_{PD2}$) means:

$$\pi^*_{PD1} = \frac{\alpha - \mu}{\beta + \theta} = \frac{\alpha + \alpha\lambda - \mu}{\beta + \dfrac{1}{\pi_{PD(OPT)}}\alpha\lambda + \theta} = \pi^*_{PD2}$$

$$(\alpha - \mu)\left(\beta + \frac{1}{\pi_{PD(OPT)}}\alpha\lambda + \theta\right) = (\alpha + \alpha\lambda - \mu)(\beta + \theta)$$

$$\alpha\beta + \alpha\frac{1}{\pi_{PD(OPT)}}\alpha\lambda + \alpha\theta - \mu\beta - \mu\frac{1}{\pi_{PD(OPT)}}\alpha\lambda - \mu\theta = \alpha\beta + \alpha\theta + \alpha\lambda\beta + \alpha\lambda\theta - \mu\beta - \mu$$

$$\alpha\frac{1}{\pi_{PD(OPT)}}\alpha\lambda - \mu\frac{1}{\pi_{PD(OPT)}}\alpha\lambda = \alpha\lambda\beta + \alpha\lambda\theta$$

$$\alpha\frac{1}{\pi_{PD(OPT)}} - \mu\frac{1}{\pi_{PD(OPT)}} = \beta + \theta$$

$$\frac{1}{\pi_{PD(OPT)}} = \frac{\beta + \theta}{\alpha - \mu}$$

$$\pi_{PD(OPT)} = \frac{\alpha - \mu}{\beta + \theta} = \pi^*_{PD1} = \pi^*_{PD2}$$

But the individual is satisficing, meaning $\pi^*_{PD1} = \pi^*_{PD2} < \pi_{PD(OPT)}$ and so this is proof by contradiction.

This also shows that when the individual is already optimising, an increase in the value of α has no effect on the allocation of the cognitive resource to this particular decision.

QED

Proposition 2

Consider the case where an increase in β from β_1 to β_2 (and so $\beta_1 < \beta_2$) causes the efficient allocation of the cognitive resource to the particular decision to either remain the same or fall:

$$\pi^*_{PD1} = \frac{\alpha - \mu}{\beta_1 + \theta} \geq \pi^*_{PD2} = \frac{\alpha - \mu}{\beta_2 + \theta}$$

$$(\alpha - \mu)(\beta_2 + \theta) \geq (\alpha - \mu)(\beta_1 + \theta)$$

$$\beta_2 + \theta \geq \beta_1 + \theta$$

$$\beta_2 \geq \beta_1$$

Again, this is a contradiction, thereby proving the proposition.

QED

Proposition 3

The proof is analogous to that for proposition 2.

QED

Propositions 4, 5 and 6

The proof of the first part of each of these propositions is the same as that for propositions 1, 2 and 3, respectively. The proof of the second part of each involves consideration of how total expected regret, given by the right-hand side of equation (6.3), alters in response to each of the changes. Assuming decisions only become more important over time, the only situation in which it is rational to procrastinate is that in which either the cognitive resources required to make the decision optimally falls, or in which the ratio of Π/Ψ_A increases, over time. In other words, in which either the direct or opportunity cost of making the decision falls over the period for which it is delayed. This analysis also suggests that it is rational for an individual to take a rest during a day if the reduction in the regret from making future decisions more optimally exceeds the costs of procrastination.

QED

Index

For Product Safety Concerns and Information please contact our EU
representative GPSR@taylorandfrancis.com
Taylor & Francis Verlag GmbH, Kaufingerstraße 24, 80331 München, Germany

www.ingramcontent.com/pod-product-compliance
Ingram Content Group UK Ltd.
Pitfield, Milton Keynes, MK11 3LW, UK
UKHW021609240425
457818UK00018B/464

9 781138 499744